Business Case Essentials

A Guide to Structure and Content

Marty J. Schmidt

Published by Solution Matrix Ltd.

Business Case Essentials, Third Edition.

International Standard Book Number: 978-1-929500-02-4

Published by Solution Matrix Ltd.
37 Wall Street, N° 25G
New York NY 10005 USA

1st Edition September 1998
2nd Edition July 2006
3rd Edition July 2009

Financial Metrics Pro and Financial Modeling Pro are trademarks of Solution Matrix Ltd.
Excel is a trademark of Microsoft Corporation.
Crystal Ball ® is a registered trademark of Oracle Corporation.

Contents

Acknowledgements

Business Case Essentials first appeared in 1998 as a 20-page white paper. It was a response to requests from consulting clients and seminar participants for a concise outline of business case structure and content. What they wanted especially was a brief, clear outline showing what belongs in a business case and why. There are many templates and examples available that show one approach or another to business case analyses for specific situations—IT hardware acquisitions, environmental protection projects, or process reeingeneering initiatives, for instance. However, none of these really bring out the essence of business case analysis itself, or what it takes "make" the case. Nor is there much available in the form of a step-by-step guidance for building and using a case. *Business Case Essentials* was written to meet those needs.

Based on reader feedback and suggestions, *Essentials* was expanded into a longer white paper in 2006, and now into a 100-page book. The goal is still to create a guide that is concise and clear, but the longer format allows more complete coverage of important questions that could not be addressed in the shorter white papers. In addition, there are many improvements due to contributions from colleagues, seminar participants, clients, and readers of all kinds.

In preparing this edition I am especially grateful for contributions and feedback from my colleagues and partners in Solution Matrix, Jeff Jackson (Auckland, New Zealand), Johannes Ritter (Frankfurt, Germany) and Anuar Mohd Ariff (Kuala Lumpur, Malaysia).

For valuable contributions, suggestions, and feedback I would also like to thank,

- Joe Ahern, Cheyenne, Wyoming
- Lars Björkeson, Stockholm, Sweden
- Allan Castillo, Irving, Texas
- Patrick Dugan, Rochester, New York
- Jörgen Eklund, Stockholm, Sweden
- Phil Lori, Perth, Australia
- Sean McSpaden, Salem, Oregon
- Tom Richardson, Santa Rosa, California
- Frank Röttgers, Frankfurt, Germany
- Don Schwartz, Santa Rosa, California
- Darren Wellington, Salem, Oregon

Marty J. Schmidt, MBA, PhD
New York, New York
8 July 2009

Chapter 1
What's a Business Case?

Essential Elements

When is a business case complete? What makes it compelling and credible? Are there standards or rules for business case structure and content? If you are asking questions like these, you are not alone. Business people today are rapidly losing tolerance for management error and, at the same time, demanding real accountability for decisions and plans. Throughout the business world, moreover, the competition for scarce funds is becoming more intense. As a result, everyone talks about the "business case" these days. Nevertheless, surprisingly few people in business really know what that means.

A business case is similar in some ways to a legal case presented in court. The trial lawyer and the business case author are both free to structure arguments, select or ignore evidence, and package the formal presentation. Whether or not the result is effective depends on their ability to tell a convincing story with compelling logic and facts. This can usually be done in many different ways. There is no single correct outline, format, or content list.

Looking beyond superficialities, however, all good cases clearly have many characteristics in common. Good business cases, for instance, always present (in one way or another) rules for deciding which data belong in the case and which do not. They stipulate, that is, the boundaries of the analysis. Readers need this information in order to know confidently that the case reflects all costs and benefits that are relevant and only those that are relevant. When fundamental information of that sort is missing or unclear, intelligent readers sense the lack instinctively and credibility suffers.

We cannot prescribe a single outline or template for all cases, but we can identify "building blocks" of this kind that are essential to building a logical structure and supporting it with evidence that will stand up to critical scrutiny, serve as a useful guide to management, and predict what actually happens.

In this book, essential building blocks appear in five categories::

- Introduction and Overview (Chapter 2)
- Assumptions and Methods (Chapter 3)
- Business Results (Chapter 4)
- Sensitivity and Risk Analysis (Chapter 5)
- Conclusions and Recommendations (Chapter 6)

This list shows a very natural order for presenting important information categories in the case. Each category, moreover, includes a number of building blocks that should be approached in a certain order. Order is important because later blocks depend on earlier blocks. In the case building project, the author develops these blocks in about the same order they appear in the business case report. In a sense, the business case author takes readers through the same reasoning—down the same path—that he or she has just traveled in building the case. You can think of *Business Case Essentials* as a journey down this path where we review what author and reader need to know about each building block.

Start With a Subject and a Purpose

The entire business case follows from a clearly described *subject* and *purpose*. In fact, we meet these two sets of information in Chapter 2, as essential building blocks in the **Introduction Section**. A subject statement describes what the case is about, and the purpose statement explains what it will be used for.

The Subject: What the Case is About

There are many kinds of business cases on many subjects, but most have this in common: Each case is "about" two kinds of things:

- A proposed action or decision.
- Meeting business objectives addressed by the action.

The business case asks "What happens if we take this or that action?" The case answers in business terms—terms focused on financial results, business objectives, and measures of progress towards those objectives. The case is "about" meeting business objectives through a proposed decision or action.

Case building begins when the case builder knows the business objectives to be addressed. These might include, for instance, reducing costs, improving employee productivity, or increasing sales revenues. Case building continues when the case builder explains how these objectives will be addressed, through specific actions such as funding a project, making a capital acquisition, or bringing a product or service to market.

Each of these potential actions presents management with choices, such as : "Should we undertake employee training? Should we fund the project? Bring the product to market? Make the acquisition? Which vendor should we choose? Should we start now or start a year from now? For such questions, the author recommends some answers over others and then "makes the case" by showing why the recommended answers are preferred.

Business Case Purpose

Why is the case being built? Who will use it? For what purpose? What information do they need in order to meet that purpose? The author needs to answer these questions before building the case because they are crucial to knowing what to put in the case.

Business people turn to the business case for several kinds of reasons:

- To address **decision support** questions, such as "Should we fund the proposed project?"
- To address **planning** questions, such as "How much funding will we need if we approve the project?"
- For **management and control** questions, such as "How do we maximize returns and minimize risks?"
- For **accountability** questions, such as "How do we show that we complied with vendor selection requirements?"

A single business case may in fact address several or all of these kinds of questions. In the current business climate such questions are coming more and more often, with increasing urgency, in business, non profit, and government organizations of all kinds.

Defining Success

From the start of the case building effort, the author needs to have in mind a clear definition for "success" with the case. To the project manager seeking project approval with a business case, getting a "Yes" from the Project Management Office might seem like success. To the sales person supporting a customer proposal with a business case, getting closure on the sale might seem like success. However, a better definition of success—one that provides practical guidance to case builder and reviewer alike—takes the position of the organization and decision makers responsible for using case results. From this viewpoint, a *successful* business case meets these criteria:

- **Credibility:** The case is believed.
- **Practical Value:**
  It enables decision makers and planners to act with confidence.
  It enables them to manage the action for optimum results.
  It discriminates clearly between proposals that should be implemented and those that should not.
- **Accuracy**: It predicts what actually happens.

Notice that these criteria are tested in the order given. If the case is not believed, the other criteria do not matter. If it does not bring decision makers to a confidence level where they will take action, no one will ever know if the predictions are accurate. Whether or not the project managers or sales people actually get approval or closure depends on their ability to design and build a case that meets these criteria.

Credibility

Business case reviewers may know a lot or they may know very little about what to look for in a business case. They may or may not know what makes the difference between a strong case and weak case. In all cases, however, you can be sure they know this much: The business case looks into the future. Everyone knows that predictions about the future come with uncertainty.

Reviewers will have questions that must be addressed–questions like these:

- How do we know we will actually see these results?
- How likely are *other* results?
- How do we know that all important costs and benefits are included?
- Are there any hidden costs or other unpleasant surprises coming?
- How do we know that different action proposals were compared fairly?

Case builders cannot hope to eliminate all uncertainty from predicted results. They are predicting the future, after all. However, they can minimize uncertainty and measure what remains. Almost all of the "building blocks" in the following chapters contribute to case credibility by providing concrete answers to the questions above. The **cost model**, for instance, helps show that all relevant costs and only the relevant costs are included (Chapter 3). **Risk analysis** shows the likelihood of other results instead of the primary predicted results (Chapter 5)

Practical Value

Business case reviewers may believe every word and number in the case, but still find the case does not meet their needs. When this happens, they may send it back to the author for re-work or more research in areas *they* are interested in. Or they may ask for stronger arguments in favor of projected results. Or, they may simply table the case and take no action on it. When this happens, the case clearly has not given reviewers enough confidence to act upon the results. For them, the case fails the practical value criterion.

Case builders can build in practical value by determining at the start of the case building project specifically:

- Which decision criteria are important to reviewers—which criteria will turn their decision one way or another.
- Which financial outcomes and which non financial outcomes reviewers are looking for.
- Other important factors that may influence reviewer decisions (e.g., mandatory legal requirements or a cash flow shortage).
- Specific information that planners need (e.g., total capital costs, or payback period for an investment).
- How competing proposals will be prioritized (the criteria by which competitors will be ranked).
- How much uncertainty reviewers are willing to accept in projected results.

First-time case builders are sometimes surprised to learn that these points are not necessarily determined or obvious when a proposed action is simply named. What it takes to "make the case" for any proposal typically depends on such things as the current business situation, the values and priorities of individual reviewers, organizational policy and history, and—most importantly—the business objectives addressed by the action.

In the business case structure presented here, the information that gives practical value to the case is identified when case building starts and is presented in the case report as part of the **purpose statement** building block (Chapter 2).

Accuracy

Failure on the first two success criteria (credibility and practical value) may disappoint the case builder. Failure on the third criterion—accuracy—can hurt the entire organization, especially if reality turns out much worse than predicted. When products fail in the market, when projects are grossly over budget, or when expensive assets do not justify their existence, the problem very likely started with an inaccurate business case.

Some people may object at this point: "It takes *time* to test accuracy. We are projecting business results three years into the future, after all (or five years, or twenty years). We won't know how the case scores on accuracy until the end of that period." And, putting the spotlight on business case accuracy makes some people uncomfortable. They ask if they should be held accountable in three years for delivering on predictions made today. "Things change," they say, "and assumptions underlying the case today will certainly be different in three years." The knowledgeable case builder has two good responses to that line of reasoning.

First, some of the case building blocks in the following chapters enable the case builder to minimize, limit, measure, and communicate uncertainty in projected business results before a proposal is implemented. The only *absolute* certainty in predicting business results is that no one can predict with absolute certainty the consequences of a complex action. If you project five-year cash flow benefits of, say, $10.5 million, you can be very sure that over time it will not be *exactly* that.

Nevertheless, the case builder can use building blocks such as the **scope and boundaries statement**, **cost model**, **benefits rationale**, **sensitivity analysis**, and **risk analysis**, to make compelling support for claims like these: "The 90% confidence interval for five-year net cash flow is $8.0 - $13.2 million." Or, "The probability that next year's training costs exceed $120 thousand is less than 0.05."

There is also an important second point about building in and communicating accuracy as well. The business case user can in fact begin testing, maintaining, and improving accuracy of case results immediately after the proposed action begins. Used this way, the business case provides a very powerful kind of statistical quality control for projects, programs, asset management, and other business investments. The key to understanding how this works is understanding the role of *assumptions* in projected business costs and benefits (See Chapter 5).

Scenarios Make the Case

Where in the business case, exactly, is the *proof* that one proposed action represents the best available business decision?

Business case proof is built on reasoning very similar to the rationale behind scientific proof in the laboratory. In chemistry or physics research, for instance, the scientist tests the idea that one factor causes another, or that one theory accounts for reality better than another, with a controlled experiment. The researcher demonstrates "proof" by comparing experimental results from different, carefully controlled test conditions.

Similarly, the business case author "proves" that one proposal or another is the best choice by comparing carefully designed *scenarios*. Generally speaking, a scenario is an account, or story, that describes what happens under one course of action. In the business case, the "what happens" is presented in business terms that are important to decision makers and planners (See "Practical Value," p. 4).

Consider briefly, an example used throughout this book referring to a company that designs and manufactures mechanical parts for aerospace industry companies. In the current economic climate, and in a highly competitive market, management decides that several business objectives are especially important:

- Reducing design and manufacturing costs.
- Improving their ability to design and produce more complex products.
- Increasing the number of products developed and sold each year.
- Increasing average gross margin per product and overall gross profits.
- Reducing new product design time.
- Reducing manufacturing setup time.

They may consider ways to address this set of objectives, such as

- Specialized training for engineering and manufacturing professionals.
- Reorganizing design teams.
- Upgrading the engineering design system software.

Which of these is the best course of action? Should they try one solution or a combination of these? A business case can address these questions by projecting and comparing business results under several action scenarios, for example:

- Scenario 1: Proposed upgrade of design system software.
- Scenario 2: Combination proposal: Train, reorganize, and upgrade software
- Scenario 3: Business as usual.

Exhibit 1-1 (next page) summarizes the structure and contents of the business case. The entire case is a logical structure, an assembly of building blocks, each designed to help establish the credibility, practical value, and accuracy of the scenarios at its heart. Based on the scenario comparison and risk and sensitivity analyses, the author will recommend one scenario for action (which may even be the "Business as Usual" scenario). The following chapters present the structure and the blocks that make this possible.

Business Case Analysis
Proposed Engineering and Manufacturing Improvements

- Subject of the case:
  - Business objectives.
  - Proposed actions.
- Purpose of the case.
  - Who will use the case and for what purpose.
  - What information is required to meet the case purpose.
- Scope and boundaries of the case.
  - Time period to be analyzed.
  - Whose costs and whose benefits are included in the case.
- Background situation and context: Why meeting these objectives is important.
- Threats and constraints impacting choice of action.
- Important assumptions and methods.
  - Benefits rationale.
  - Cost model.
  - Assumptions (e.g., market size, inflation rate, raw materials prices).
- Proposed action scenarios.

Scenario 3: Business as Usual (Baseline)

Scenario 2: Combination Proposal

Scenario 1: Proposed Upgrade Design System Software

- Scenario-specific actions
- Scenario-specific assumptions
- Projected financial results

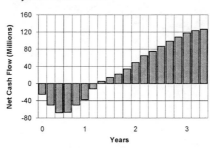

- Financial metrics (e.g., total cost, net cash flow, net present value, return on investment, and payback period)
- Non financial benefits and costs (contributions to non financial business objectives)

- Scenario results compared.
- Sensitivity analysis: (measures how much each assumption contributes to business results).
- Risk analysis (the likelihood of different outcomes).
- Conclusions and Recommendations.
  - Recommended choice of action scenario.
  - Critical success factors, important contingencies, and risk factors that must be watched.

Exhibit 1-1. Business case structure and content.

Chapter 1 Summary

- There is no single correct outline or content for the business case, but all good cases have some characteristics (building blocks and structure) in common.

- Essential building blocks for the case naturally fall into five categories:
  - Introduction and overview
  - Assumptions and methods
  - Business results
  - Sensitivity and risk analysis
  - Conclusions and recommendations

- The business case subject statement describes what the case is about. The proposed actions are described, and the business objectives they address are presented. The subject statement also identifies the different action scenarios that will be compared.

- The business case purpose statement describes who will use the case, for what purpose, and what information they need to meet that purpose.

- A successful business case meets these criteria:
  - Credibility: The case is believed.
  - Practical value: It enables decision makers and planners to act with confidence.
  - Accuracy: It predicts what actually happens.

- The author makes the case ("proves") that one scenario represents the better business decision by comparing projected results from two or more action scenarios. Insofar as possible, one of these will be a "Business as Usual" (baseline) scenario.

Chapter 2

Introduction and Overview

Most of these blocks must be completed before other parts of case design can proceed, especially the Subject and Purpose Statements. The Executive Summary is the only exception to this rule. It will be written last but read first by the audience. In any case, some of the audience may read only these parts. Obviously these building blocks need to represent the entire case in terms that are terse, clear, and accurate.

Business Case Structure
A. Introduction
B. Methods and Assumptions
C. Business Results
D. Sensitivity and Risk Analysis
E. Conclusions and Recommendations

A. INTRODUCTION

- **Title and Subtitle**
- **Authors and Recipients**
- **Date**
- **Executive Summary**
- **Disclaimer**
- **Subject:**
  What the case is about: Business objectives and proposed actions.
- **Purpose:**
  Why the case exists and what it will be used for, what information it needs.
- **Situation:**
  Opportunities, threats, problems, limitations and constraints that put the case in context and show why meeting the business objectives is important.

Title and Subtitle

A good business case **title** briefly identifies the proposed action and the general nature of the analysis. For example:

- Business Case Analysis: Proposed Engineering and Manufacturing Improvements.
- Proposed Server System Upgrades: Total Cost of Ownership Analysis.
- Cost/Benefit Study of Proposed Employee Recreation Facility

Other terms for the general nature of the case might include:

- Business impact study
- Return on investment analysis
- Feasibility study
- Financial justification analysis
- Projected cash flow impact
- Business benefits analysis

A title is essential, of course, but you may also have the option of adding a **subtitle** to let readers know more fully what the case is about. A subtitle can add interest and clarity by identifying up front such things as:

- The time period analyzed.
  "Financial Projections for Fiscal 2010–2012"

- The specific action considered for analysis (when several actions ave been proposed).
  "October 2009 upgrade proposal from Avanti Systems"

- Special characteristics of the method.
  "Five year projections based on historical data from 2005-2009"

Subtitles should cover no more than one or two lines—otherwise they begin to take over the role of Executive Summary. Note that business case subtitles are not like the "tag lines" after titles in magazine or newspaper items. There, authors create interest by revealing conclusions or making editorial comments ("Read the fine print before you sign a service contract!"). For the formal business case, however, conclusions or editorials in the title or subtitle seem unprofessional and make the case look less objective.

Author and Recipients

Case credibility benefits when the identities of the **author** and **recipients** are given. Business cases are shaped significantly by the author's personality and by the identity and needs of the intended recipients. Case readers of all kinds know better how to evaluate the case if they know specifically who these people are. By contrast, a case apparently written by "Anonymous" and addressed to no one in particular simply does not carry the same initial credibility in the minds of readers and reviewers.

Author and recipients may appear after "To" and "From" headers, as on a formal memo. An address with both "To" and "From" is especially appropriate if the case is prepared by consultants, sales people, or anyone outside the receiving company or organization.

"To" may address an individual, in which case title and company (or organization) should be included:

To: Mr. Joseph Williams, President
     Aerofirma Aerospace Assemblies

Or, the report may be "To" (or "Prepared for" or "Submitted to") a committee or group ("Project Management Office," "Capital Review Board," or "Executive Management Committee").

This is another way that business cases differ from standard accounting reports or budgets, where authorship may or may not be known, where recipients are not named, and where credibility is rarely an issue. Readers probably do not care specifically which accountant put the final touches on the income statement, or which senior executive made the final adjustment to the capital budget ceiling. Everyone knows, however, that business cases reflect arbitrary and subjective judgements, that projections are uncertain, and that no two analysts are likely to produce exactly the same results. For credibility reasons alone, it is helpful to show who is responsible for the report. An anonymous business case would be less than compelling in most settings, no matter how good the content. Also, if the case serves later as a management tool or model for other cases, users may want to contact the author(s) or recipients for elaboration or explanation.

Authorship may also be attributed to committees or groups ("Submitted by the Project 2010 Study Committee"), which is fine, if the actual individuals can be identified elsewhere in the report, perhaps in a footnote or appendix.

The author and recipient information can also show at the outset that a number of people contributed to the content. As the head of a study group or project team, it is important to remind readers that individuals from many functional areas contributed—maybe including finance, human resources, marketing, strategic planning, line management, and so on. And, when the case is written by an outside consultant or sales person, it is important to register any contributors inside the recipient company or organization.

Date

The cover page of the case report should show the dates completed and submitted. Business cases are often revised and reissued through several cycles. Completion and submission dates on the first page make it easy to find the latest version.

Other text, especially in the "Methods" section, should indicate when the data were gathered or developed. ("Cost estimates reflect vendor prices in effect during August, 2009," or "Estimated expenses are based on customer service request patterns for the years 2006 through 2009"). This is important because cases use sources that change: business plans, prices, salary and staffing data—all change over time and all may contribute to case results. Dating the source data this way lets the audience know exactly which data were used, avoiding potential confusion later.

Executive Summary

Readers expect to find an **Executive Summary** early in the report. Though the Executive Summary may be the first text item in the report, it will be the last item written in the case-building project. It is most useful if it contains text, numbers, and at least one image of graphed results. The following, for example, makes a useful one-page Executive Summary:

- A short narrative paragraph tersely identifying the subject, scope, and methods of analysis.
- A list or table of financial metrics from the analysis for each action scenario considered (e.g., net cash flow, net present value, payback period, internal rate of return, or total cost of ownership).
- Important non financial benefits and costs for each scenario.
- A brief description of major risks, contingencies and critical success factors for the recommended action scenario.
- A bar graph showing projected incremental cash flow results (or net cash flow, or cumulative cash flow) across the analysis period.

The Executive Summary deserves careful preparation and formatting. Some of the audience will probably read *only* the executive summary. The summary is the author's one chance to reach these people. Other members of the audience will read some or all of the case report, but miss the main conclusions, misunderstand the subject and scope, or otherwise misinterpret the case—unless these elements are presented clearly in the executive summary.

The rest of the audience—even those who read the case report carefully and completely—will still want to know the essence of the whole case from the outset. It is natural to view the executive summary as the author's proposition that says, essentially, "This is what I propose to show you."

Disclaimer

Including a **disclaimer** in your report is advisable if you prepare the case for recipients outside your own company or organization. The Aerofirma CIO, writing a case for other senior executives in the same company probably would not include a disclaimer in a business case. However, an outside vendor (e.g., a systems integrator) proposing a solution to Aerofirma and supporting the proposal with a business case, probably *would* (and should) include a disclaimer. The disclaimer can help set audience expectations properly, but its primary purpose is to provide legal protection for the case developer. The message of the disclaimer is, in effect, something like this:

I built this case carefully and professionally, but ...

- Do not hold me legally responsible for the accuracy of these predictions.
- Estimates of future financial results always include some uncertainty.
- The results depend on some factors beyond my control.
- The results are based on information that may change (such as prices).
- The results may depend on important information I was unaware of.
- The results depend in part upon information you furnished to me.
- This analysis does not claim to provide professional tax guidance.

In a real business case, of course, the phrasing is more formal and diplomatic. Here, for instance, is the disclaimer used by one IT (Information Technology) system integration consultant from the firm "Avanti Integrators:"

"This report provides approximations of important financial consequences that should be considered in decisions involving the purchase, installation, and configuration of computing hardware and software. The analysis is based on information which was provided by you as well as information believed by Avanti Integrators to be accurate. Price information is subject to change at any time. We recommend that you use this analysis only as an aid to develop your own cost and benefit analyses. The actual tax impact can only be determined accurately by consultation with tax advisors."

If you suspect that a disclaimer might be advisable in your work, then check with your organization's legal department or find a qualified lawyer who can discuss your responsibilities, vulnerabilities, and potential liabilities from a legal standpoint. Verify that your disclaimer text is appropriate. And, when you use a disclaimer, either give it a text section of its own, early in the report, or set it off from other text in some unmistakable way (e.g., with a different typeface or indentation). Be sure to bring it to the attention of your audience at least once. Do not bury it in the footnotes or appendixes.

Of course, a disclaimer will not fully protect you from the legal consequences of incompetent work, misrepresenting your qualifications, or misusing case results. However, if you do your best in good faith, it can provide some protection against a client or customer who later makes unfair claims against you or your organization.

Subject Statement

Every business case needs a **subject statement,** describing what the case is about. The statement is critically important because it helps define or shape almost everything else in the case.

Two good analysts can work independently on the same subject and arrive at different business case results, but they should be very similar results if they start from the same subject statement, where actions and objectives have been defined fully in precise and concrete terms. If the subject is defined incompletely, vaguely, or imprecisely, they may arrive at quite different results. To a certain extent, the results are determined (but not yet visible) when the subject is stated properly.

The subject statement describes what is being proposed, and why, through four kinds of information. A good subject statement

- Names the proposed action or actions.
- Lists scenarios to be evaluated.
- Identifies business objectives addressed by the actions.
- Describes the main components of the proposed action.

Only when those points are fully articulated, do author and recipients really know what the case is "about."

Name the Proposed Action

Fully naming the action is little more than a very long version of the business case title, but it is an important preparation for the reader before stepping into the specific actions and objectives of the subject statement. Here, for example, is that part of the Aerofirma example case subject statement:

This case examines the likely 3-year costs and benefits to Aerofirma Aerospace Assemblies from several proposed changes within design engineering and manufacturing, intended to reduce costs, improve design abilities, and shorten design and manufacturing times. Possible changes include upgrading the engineering mechanical design software, reorganizing engineering design teams, improving engineering design and manufacturing set up processes, and providing additional, intensive training for design and manufacturing professionals.

List the Scenarios

The business case attempts to predict the future, and everyone knows that the future can work out an infinite number of ways. The business case author cannot hope to anticipate all of these possibilities. Instead, a small set of possible future scenarios will be developed and analyzed. The choice of scenarios is driven by the purpose of the business case itself (see the discussion on the **purpose statement**, the next building block, pp. 17-19). Here, the author says, "These are the choices for action."

The example Aerofirma case identifies three scenarios. At the end of the case report, the author will recommend one of these scenarios for action.

This case examines three possible scenarios for Aerofirma Corporation:

Scenario 1: Proposed Upgrade. Aerofirma's primary mechanical design engineering software system, DesignMax, will be upgraded from V7 (two dimensional design) to V9 (three dimensional), as proposed to Aerofirma by Avanti Integrators in September 2009.

Scenario 2: Combination Proposal. Engineering design software will be upgraded, as in Scenario 1, but also, engineering design groups will be reorganized, the manufacturing set up process will be improved, and engineering and manufacturing professionals will receive additional intensive training.

Scenario 3: Business as Usual. Design and manufacturing activities will continue with the current design system software, current levels of training, and the current organizational structure and processes.

Notice especially the use of Scenario 3, the "Business as Usual" scenario. Some people ask if it is necessary to include this scenario in cases where "business as usual" is not an option on the table, and a decision has already been made to "do something".

A Business as Usual scenario is always recommended, except in the most extreme situations where it might be so unrealistic as to be unthinkable. The cost and benefit estimates for the Business as Usual scenario serve as a baseline for measuring savings, improvements, reductions, and increases in the *other* scenarios. You can only demonstrate an expected cost savings in a proposal scenario, for instance, by comparing expected spending there to expected spending under the current situation.

Identify Business Objectives

Often, the trigger that starts the business case author building the case is the need to support a proposed action. Author and recipients should keep in mind, however, that actions are driven and justified by business objectives. Objectives should be identified at the start of the case report in the **subject** block. Business case analyst and business case readers alike need to know from the start *why* the actions are proposed.

The actions under analysis could be meant, for instance to

- Reduce costs.
- Meet regulatory requirements.
- Improve quality of service delivery.
- Increase sales, market share, or margins.
- Improve the organization's public image.
- Lower risks.
- Improve "branding."
- Reduce product development time and time to market.
- Improve employee morale.

And so on. Objectives for action may be high level strategic objectives ("Become the industry leader in customer satisfaction") or lower level operational objectives ("Reduce average customer wait time from 3 minutes to 15 seconds"). Regardless, the author's case rests on his or her ability to show that reaching these objectives has value, and that proposed actions contribute to getting there. Some of these objectives may be defined or measured first in financial terms ("reduce costs") and some in non financial terms ("improve employee morale"). In government and other public sector cases, especially, the non financial objectives may be the most important reasons for proposing action.

For the Aerofirma example case, objectives might be stated this way:

The three scenarios will be compared on the basis of measurable contributions to the following objectives:

- Improve average gross margin per product and increase company gross profits for product sales. These improvements are approached through meeting the following objectives:
  - Enable higher levels of design customization for different customers, producing products which are sold at higher margins.
  - Increase the number of products developed and sold each year, through improved design engineer productivity and reduced product development time.
- Reduce design costs in change management.
- Avoid hiring costs for additional design engineers, which will otherwise be needed over the next three years.

The subject statement simply names the business objectives targeted by proposed actions. Later, in the **Purpose** statement, **Situation,** and **Benefits Rationale** blocks the author must explain how progress towards these objectives is measured, set target levels for the objectives, and explain why they are important.

If you think of the business case as a cost/benefit analysis, most "benefits" from any proposed action will come from meeting objectives. Actions (the next part of the subject statement) bring costs or cost savings.

Describe the Proposed Actions

Once business objectives are identified, the next, equally important part of the subject statement presents the proposed actions.

As suggested, the case title should briefly identify the proposed action ("Proposed Engineering and Manufacturing Improvements" or "Proposed Marketing Campaign," for instance). The subject statement scenario list (p. 14) describes at a very high level which actions are included in each scenario. Now, however, the proposed actions must be described at the next level of detail. Only when all the major components of proposed actions are in view, do the author and recipients know fully what the analysis covers.

Business case analysis is applied to many kinds of actions, for instance:

- A capital acquisition.
- An infrastructure upgrade or equipment replacement.
- A construction project.
- An engineering design project.
- An investment in new capabilities or capacity.
- Bringing a product or service to market.
- A change in organization or operations.
- A move into a new market.

This list shows how the actions might appear in the title, or scenario list, but a little thought about what has to be done in each case to achieve business objectives, shows that each of these is really a collection of many actions. In Aerofirma's Scenario 1, the Proposed Upgrade scenario, the major components of that proposed action might be described as follows:

Scenario 1: Proposed Upgrade. Aerofirma's primary mechanical design engineering software system, DesignMax, will be upgraded from V7 (two dimensional design) to V9 (three dimensional).

In order to meet business objectives for this action, Aerofirma must:

- Develop and implement a 1-year software migration plan.
- Purchase 40 user copies of the DesignMax engineering design module.
- Purchase the DesignMax design data base module.
- Design and create a new design data base and migrate existing data.
- Upgrade engineering desktop systems, increase server system capacity, and double current disk storage space.
- Contract systems integration work from outside contractors.
- Implement design system transition with no delay of projects in progress.
- Train design engineers on upgraded systems.
- Train IT support staff to maintain and service the upgraded system.
- Prepare manufacturing systems to accept and implement new design data.

A similar list would have to be included for the Scenarios 2, and 3. For Scenario 2 (the Combination Proposal), the action list would be longer, because it includes everything proposed for Scenario 1 plus all the actions required to bring about the reorganization, changes to manufacturing set up, and additional professional training. And, even Scenario 3 (Business as usual) requires action statements like those above, indicating what is planned in each area (or not planned) if neither scenario 1 or 2 is implemented.

People sometimes ask just how many action components need to be listed here, and at what level of detail. There is no good universal answer, except to say that the author should be sure to name every major action component that will bring significant costs, or which has to be completed in the overall action, or which may bring risks to the successful implementation. If an important action item is omitted here, the author seriously risks under estimating costs and over estimating the probability of success with the proposal. If an important action item is omitted here, the author also risks having to return to the funding source, later, with a request for additional funding.

Purpose Statement

The need for a subject statement and its role may be obvious, even to those who are new to business case analysis. There is another set of preliminary information, however, whose importance may be less obvious to business case newcomers. The subject statement describes the purpose of the proposed actions, but a few statements about the purpose of the business case itself are also critically important to author and recipients alike. The content of the case and the author's recommendations and conclusions may depend heavily on the purpose of the case.

The general purpose may be to support decision making and planning but the developer needs to know specifically, and communicate in the report:

- Who will use the case.
- What decision or plan the case supports.
- What kinds of information recipients require.

A **purpose statement**, developed when case building starts, and positioned early in the report, should address each of these points.

Remember that the case will be read and used by *individuals*. Different people—even in same organization—may differ substantially in priorities, decision criteria, motivation, and tolerance for risk.

Different uses of the case may also call for different kinds of information and different interpretations of the results. The business case author needs to know, from the start, how the case will be used. Business cases are used for many purposes, including for example:

- **Decision support** to address questions like these:
  - Which products should we bring to market?
  - Should we fund the proposed project?
  - Which contractor should we choose to provide service?
  - Should we lease the service vehicles or buy them?
  - Which capital acquisition proposals should we approve?
  - Should we approve a proposal that requires non-budgeted funds?
  - Does implementing the proposal represent a good business decision?

- **Planning** questions such as these:
  If we undertake the action:
  – How much funding will we need?
  – What does our capital budget need to be?
  – What will the marketing program contribute to sales revenues?

- **Management and control** questions such as:
  – How do we maximize returns and minimize risk?
  – Where are the greatest risks of cost overruns?
  – Which critical success factors must we manage, to what target levels, to achieve projected results?

- **Accountability** purposes to address questions like these:
  – How do we show in 3 years that decisions we make today are good business decisions based on the information we have now?
  – How do we show that we complied with vendor selection requirements?

A single business case, in fact, may be undertaken for several or all of these purposes. If one purpose is to decide whether or not a project proposal is a good business decision for the organization, for instance, and another purpose is to determine how much funding is required for the project, the case must deliver information that meets both purposes.

Obviously, the case purpose impacts the author's choice of scenarios as well as the choice of business results to project for each scenario. To complete the purpose statement, the author should list specifically which financial and non financial information will be delivered for case scenarios.

A purpose statement in the business case report should be succinct but complete. Some of the information here (the scenario list) necessarily repeats some of the subject statement. For example:

This analysis and report are prepared for the members of Aerofirma Executive Management Committee, who will meet in December 2009 to decide whether or not to implement upgrades to Aerofirma's primary engineering software system and other proposed changes in the Engineering and Manufacturing organizations. Options for action include three scenarios evaluated in this case:

1. Proposed Scenario: Upgrade engineering design software system.
2. Combination Proposal: Upgrade design software, reorganize engineering workgroups, improve manufacturing set up process, provide additional professional training.
3. Business as Usual (implement none of the proposed actions).

In choosing a course of action, the Executive Committee will give special attention to these projected financial and non financial results under all scenarios:

Financial metrics based on estimated cash inflows and outflows

- Total 3 year costs.
- Cost reductions, especially in change management, design process time, and manufacturing set up.
- Net cash flow and net incremental cash flow results from project investments.
- 3-year net present value (NPV) of project investments.
- 3-year return on investment (ROI).

Marketing, sales, operational, and performance metrics

- Increase in gross margins, coming from greater design capabilities.
- Average order size expected from Aerofirma's largest customer accounts.
- Average design time for products at current complexity levels and at higher levels.
- Average manufacturing set up time.

Risks and other factors
- Risks to achieving improvements in gross profits targets.
- Risks to timely completion of work in progress.
- The likelihood of grossly exceeding cost estimates.
- The likelihood that learning curves will be longer than anticipated.

Important business decisions should rarely be made on the basis of just one financial metric or decision criterion. Aerofirma management will of course give higher priority to some of these measures than others, but they will want to consider all of them when deciding which scenario to implement.

The Situation

Good business case writing—like good journalism—maintains a clear distinction between direct factual reporting, on the one hand, and editorializing and interpretations on the other. The business case calls for both kinds of writing, but readers must be able to see clearly which is which in the report. Whereas the **subject** and **purpose** statements are more or less bare bone statements of fact, the **Situation** block gives the author a much-needed opportunity to present and interpret the context for these statements.

In brief, the Situation block should show why the objectives addressed by proposals are important, and anything else the audience needs to know about the current business situation, risks, or company/organizational strengths and weaknesses, in order to understand this. This is the place for what is sometimes called SWOT analysis (strengths, weaknesses, opportunities, and threats). When authors make recommendations and draw conclusions at the end of the report, they will refer to reasoning developed here, in the Situation block, to "make" the case.

The Situation block can serve this purpose by addressing questions like these:

- **Business Objectives**
  - Why are the objectives from the subject statement important? How do they contribute to company or organization strengths?
  - How do we measure progress towards each objective? How do we make the objective and progress towards it tangible?
  - What are the target levels for each objective?
  - How do these objectives represent opportunities?
  - How will the proposed action contribute to reaching targets?
  - Where do we stand now on meeting these objectives?
  - What is the financial value of reaching the targets?

- **Strategic Importance**
  - Which of the organization's strategic (high level) objectives do the proposed actions support?
  - Which higher level objectives are supported by lower level objectives? A lower level objective to "shorten service delivery time" might, for instance, support a strategic objective, "improve customer satisfaction."

- **Threats and Constraints**
  - What are the consequences or costs of *not* reaching targets for objectives?
  - How do the subject statement objectives compete or conflict with other objectives?
  - Are there important time constraints on reaching any of the objectives? (e.g., getting a product to market before the competition, or replacing equipment before it becomes obsolete, or relying on resources that will only be available during a certain time period).
  - Does the organization face increased competition in the marketplace?
  - Is the competition for scarce funds increasing?
  - Does the organization have a cash flow shortage or other financial problems?
  - Do the proposed actions address current legal liabilities or legal vulnerabilities?

- **Relevant History**
  - Is there a previous history in the organization of similar proposals?
  - Were previous similar proposals approved or supported? If not, why not?
  - Are there important learnings from previous actions that help identify opportunities or risks associated with the current proposal?

- **The Rationale for Decision Options and Scenario Choices**
  - The Subject Statement names one or more action scenarios presented for evaluation in the business case. Why were these scenarios chosen?
  - Were there other action choices considered but then rejected for inclusion? If so, why?

Why were *these* specific scenarios selected as the only choices for action to consider? Addressing this question at the end of the Situation block makes a natural transition into the following Methods section, where the scenarios and the major assumptions behind them are developed.

Chapter 2 Summary

Business Case Structure
A. Introduction
B. Methods and Assumptions
C. Business Results
D. Sensitivity and Risk Analysis
E. Conclusions and Recommendations

A. INTRODUCTION

- **Title and Subtitle**
- **Authors and Recipients**
- **Date**
- **Executive Summary**
- **Disclaimer**
- **Subject:**
  What the case is about: Business objectives and proposed actions.
- **Purpose:**
  Why the case exists and what it will be used for, what information it needs.
- **Situation:**
  Opportunities, threats, problems, limitations and constraints that put the case in context and show why meeting the business objectives is important.

- A good business case title briefly identifies the proposed action and the general nature of the analysis.

- A subtitle can add interest and clarity to the title, such as "Financial projections for Fiscal 2010 - 2012."

- Case credibility benefits when the identities of the author and recipients are given.

- Business cases are often revised through several iterations. In addition, much of the data in the case is based on sources that are continually updated. For those reasons, the business case report should indicate the date completed and the dates of data sources.

- The Executive Summary should present the whole case in miniature. Some readers will read only the Executive Summary. Even those who carefully read the entire case still need to be told in the Executive Summary what they will find there, and what the author intends to show.

- A disclaimer is advisable if the case is prepared for an audience outside the author's company or organization.

- The business case subject statement describes what the case is about. The proposed actions are described, and the business objectives they address are presented. The subject statement also identifies the different action scenarios that will be compared.

- The business case purpose statement describes who will use the case, for what purpose, and what information they need to meet that purpose.

- The Situation block shows *why* the objectives addressed by proposals are important, and anything else the audience needs to know about the current business situation, risks, or company/organizational strengths and weaknesses.

Chapter 3
Methods and Assumptions

The business case analysis predicts financial and non financial outcomes for each action scenario in the case. The strength of the case and case credibility depend heavily on the author's ability to show where the data and results come from. Essential building blocks in this section serve that purpose.

Where should this information appear in the case report? The natural place for a Methods and Assumptions Section is right after the Introduction and before Business Results. If the material is very long, however, it is better divided into two sections: A shorter section, covering key assumptions and an overview of methodology appearing before Business Results, with a longer section spelling out assumptions and methods completely in an appendix.

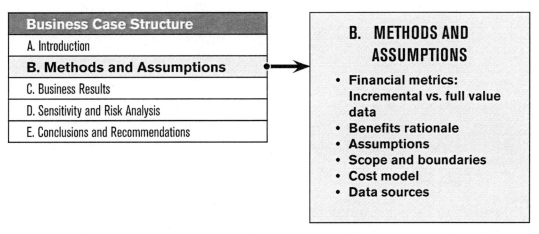

What will it take for the case to accomplish its purpose? What information do readers need in order to make decisions or plans? These questions were raised in the **Purpose Statement** (pp. 17-19), and answered there with a list of financial metrics and other business outcomes. The blocks in the **Methods Section** spell out how that information is developed and how it will be used. Put another way, this section sets the rules for what belongs in the case and what does not. This section also *legitimizes* specific cost and benefit items for the case.

Some readers may skip the **Methods Section** entirely and head straight for the "bottom line" outcomes in the next section, **Business Results**. However, the critical reader, the responsible decision maker, the careful Chief Financial Officer, and any others who want to decide for themselves whether or not they agree with the author's recommendations and conclusions, will not automatically accept the results until they see where they come from. For this reason, the "Methods Section" might also be called the Credibility Section.

Financial Metrics

Most business case analyses include both financial and non-financial business outcomes, whether the setting is a profit-making company, a government organization, or a non-profit entity.

The financial component is nearly always present because almost any proposed action, in any setting, brings financial costs of some kind. These enter the analysis as projected *cash outflows*. The case may or may not include financial benefits, which enter the analysis as projected *cash inflows,* coming from such things as sales revenues or cost savings for instance, but also from expected results that can be assigned financial value, such as improved productivity. Cash inflows and outflows are brought together in **Cash Flow Statements** in the **Business Results** section. These, in turn, provide the basis for further analyses, including financial metrics such as *total cost, net present value* (NPV) and *return on investment* (ROI).

Case builders and case readers are well served if the author includes a **Methods Section** block called **Financial Metrics** to illustrate the structure of the financial model and the kinds of cash flow data that will produce financial metrics. Including this block is good practice, because there are several "traps" or stumbling blocks that can—and often do—confuse people reviewing business case financial results (see the list of potential confusions on page 27).

Exhibits 3.1 (next page) and 3.2 (p. 26) show how this section might look in a typical simple two-scenario case. Remember that readers will probably use information of this kind to decide which option (Proposal or Business as Usual) is the better business decision. They may also use it to address planning questions such as "If we implement the proposal, what does our operating budget need to be?" Note that cash flow numbers appear in these exhibits simply to help illustrate calculations. Real business case results appear later in the **Business Results Section.**

Exhibit 3.1 shows the general structure of the cash flow statements: For each scenario, the author looks forward in time, estimating cash outflows (costs) or cash inflows (benefits) for each cost and benefit item in the case.

The distinction between *full value* and *incremental* figures is especially important. The upper two panels in Exhibit 3.1 show the estimated inflows and outflows at full value: The full Year 1 cash outflow for Cost Item E, for instance, is expected to be 35 under the Proposal Scenario and 25 under Business as Usual. That kind of information is useful for predicting funding needs and developing budgets.

The incremental cash flow statement, however, shows line-item-by-line item *differences* between the two scenarios. When the Proposal Scenario is compared to Business as Usual, Cost item E cash outflow increases by 10 in Year 1 under the Proposal. This is the increment, or Δ, between scenarios for this item. Exhibit 2.2 (previous page) illustrates the incremental calculations. Incremental comparisons of this kind are especially helpful for deciding which scenario is the better course of action.

Notice also the sign convention used in all three panels of Exhibit 3.1. All expected cash inflows are positive numbers and all expected outflows appear in parentheses to show they are negative numbers. The author who uses this convention and makes a careful distinction between full value and incremental figures, helps avoid potential confusion in several ways:

PROPOSAL SCENARIO, FULL VALUE CF

	Yr 1	Yr 2	Yr 3	Total
Benefits				
Benefit A.........	155	175	220	550
Benefit B........	135	160	190	485
Total Benefits	290	335	410	1,035
Costs				
Cost C............	(45)	(55)	(65)	(165)
Cost D...........	(75)	(75)	(80)	(230)
Cost E...........	(35)	(30)	(40)	(105)
Total Costs	(155)	(160)	(185)	(500)
Net Cash Flow	135	175	225	**535**
Cumulative CF.....	135	310	535	
Disc.CF @8%......	125	150	179	454

BUSINESS AS USUAL SCENARIO, FULL VALUE CF

	Yr 1	Yr 2	Yr 3	Total
Benefits				
Benefit A.........	140	170	200	510
Benefit B........	135	150	165	450
Total Benefits	275	320	365	960
Costs				
Cost C............	(50)	(70)	(85)	(205)
Cost D...........	(60)	(65)	(65)	(190)
Cost E...........	(25)	(30)	(35)	(90)
Total Costs	(135)	(165)	(185)	(485)
Net Cash Flow	140	155	180	**475**
Cumulative CF.....	140	295	475	
Disc.CF @8%......	130	133	143	405

INCREMENTAL CASH FLOW

	Yr 1	Yr 2	Yr 3	Total	
Benefits					
Benefit A increase	15	5	20	40	
Benefit B increase	0	10	25	35	
Cost C Savings....	5	15	20	40	
Total Ben. Increase	20	30	65	115	← Incremental Benefits
Costs					
Cost D Increase....	(15)	(10)	(15)	(40)	
Cost E Incr.......	(10)	0	(5)	(15)	
Total Cost Increase	(25)	(10)	(20)	(55)	← Incremental Costs
Incremental CF	(5)	20	45	**60**	← Incremental Cash Flow
Cumul. Incr. CF	(5)	15	60		
Disc. Incr. CF @8%	(4.6)	17.1	35.7	48.2	← Net Present Value (NPV)

Exhibit 3.1 Business case financial results are derived from cash flow statements, one for each action scenario. The *full value* scenarios, above, project actual cash inflows and outflows for each cost and benefit item. The *incremental* cash flow statement, at bottom, shows only the differences between two full value scenarios.

FINANCIAL METRICS SUMMARY

- **Cash Flow**

  Cash inflows are positive numbers. Cash outflows are negative numbers with parentheses ( )

- **Incremental Cash Flow (Δ)**

  Each incremental cash flow item is the difference between two corresponding full value items: Incremental cash flow Δ = Proposal cash flow, less Business As Usual (BAU) cash flow

$$\Delta \ = \ \text{Proposal CF} - \text{BAU CF}$$

- **Incremental Cash Flow Examples (based on Exhibit 3.1, Yr 1 data)**

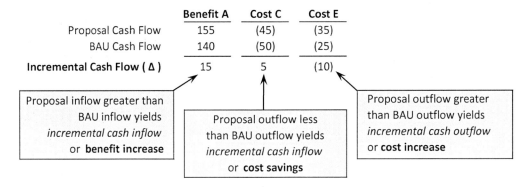

	Benefit A	Cost C	Cost E
Proposal Cash Flow	155	(45)	(35)
BAU Cash Flow	140	(50)	(25)
Incremental Cash Flow (Δ)	15	5	(10)

Proposal inflow greater than BAU inflow yields *incremental cash inflow* or **benefit increase**	Proposal outflow less than BAU outflow yields *incremental cash inflow* or **cost savings**	Proposal outflow greater than BAU outflow yields *incremental cash outflow* or **cost increase**

- **Discounted Cash Flow (DCF) and Net Present Value (NPV)**

  Discounted Cash Flow (DCF) values are based on annual net cash flow figures. Each year's discounted value (present value, PV) uses an 8% discount rate and end-of-year discounting.

$$PV_1 \ = \ \text{Net CF}_1 \ / \ (1 + 0.08)^1 \qquad \textit{Present value for Year 1}$$

$$PV_3 \ = \ \text{Net CF}_3 \ / \ (1 + 0.08)^3 \qquad \textit{Present value for Year 3}$$

$$\ = \ 45 \ / \ (1+.08)^3 \ = \ 35.7 \qquad \textit{Example Year 3 PV for incremental cash flow}$$

$$NPV \ = \ PV_1 + PV_2 + PV_3$$

- **Return on Investment (ROI)**

  Three Year Return on Investment (ROI) is calculated from Incremental cash flow figures as:

$$ROI \ = \ (\text{3-Yr Incremental Gain} - \text{3-Yr Incremental Cost}) / (\text{3-Yr Incremental Cost})$$

$$\ = \ (115 - 55) / 55 \ = \ 109.1\% \qquad \textit{Example 3-Year incremental cash flow ROI}$$

Exhibit 3.2. Financial metrics summary for the Methods Section, showing how cash flow figures from the examples.

- **Confusing plus and minus operations.** There is no question about which figures result from addition and which figures result from subtraction. With positive inflows and negative outflows, the only arithmetic operation applied to the numbers is *addition*.
- **Finding and measuring cost savings.** Cost savings under a proposal scenario appear as positive numbers—cash inflows in the incremental cash flow statement. In Exhibit 3.1 example, for instance, Cost C has been elevated legitimately into the "Benefits" section of the incremental statement because the expected cost savings are positive incremental inflows each year. Cost savings can also be seen by comparing two full value scenarios, side by side, but the incremental statement measures them directly.
- **Mixing full value and incremental data.** Presenting full value and incremental statements side by side lowers the risk of *mixing* the two kinds of data on the same statement. When an incremental cost and a full value cost are added together, for instance, the result is meaningless and misleading.

There is abundant room for confusion with financial metrics, as well: Different people can mean different things when they use terms like "ROI" or "NPV." Cash flow discounting for NPV can be done on a monthly, quarterly basis, or annual basis, for instance, using either end-of-period discounting or mid-period discounting. And, there are at least eight different ways to calculate cash flow ROI. However, examples such as Exhibit 3.2 in a **Financial Metrics** block can show everyone just how the author develops specific metrics.[1]

Finally, you may wonder how Exhibit 3.1 would look if there were two or more proposal scenarios, as in the "Aerofirma" example from the previous two chapters. In that case, the proposal Scenarios were called "Proposed Upgrade" and "Combination Proposal." When a Business as Usual scenario is included as well, the analysis calls for *five* cash flow statements, as shown in Exhibit 3.3 (next page). Both full value proposal scenarios are compared to the same Business as Usual scenario to produce incremental cash flow statements.

---

1. Business case analysis focuses on *cash flow metrics*, as illustrated here, such as NPV, ROI, and others. These metrics are calculated from projected cash flow figures, as shown. For a complete coverage of financial metrics in the business case—selection, calculation, and usage—see the *Business Case Guide* or Financial Metrics Pro™. More information on these publications can be found at www.solutionmatrix.com.

The other major class of financial metrics includes *financial ratios* (or *financial statement metrics*), such as the current ratio, inventory turns, or profitability. These are derived from financial accounting statements, primarily the income statement and balance sheet. Financial ratios of this kind enter the business case only when they, themselves, are objectives for action. A case evaluating different proposals meant to improve profitability, for instance, or proposals meant to increase inventory turns, would also attempt to predict profitability or inventory turns under different scenarios.

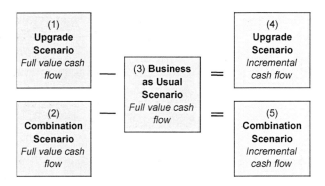

Exhibit 3.3. A case with two proposal scenarios such as the Aerofirma example shown here, needs just one Business as Usual scenario. Both proposal scenarios (1 and 2) are compared to the same Business as Usual cash flow statement (3) to produce incremental cash flow statements (4 and 5).

Benefits Rationale

Some people seem to think of "business case" and "financial case" as nearly synonymous terms. In reality, however, many business initiatives and projects target non financial objectives. The answer to the question: "Which proposal is the better business decision?" may depend on non financial criteria instead of financial criteria. Or, the decision may turn on a combination of financial and non financial outcomes. This is especially likely when the context is a government or non profit organization.

The **Financial Metrics** block shows how financial results enter the case. Here, a **Benefits Rationale** block opens the door to the complete range of benefit and cost impacts, including those that may be difficult or impossible to measure in financial terms. In brief, this block serves to legitimize all important financial and non financial business impacts for the case and show how they can be valued.

Benefits Terminology

To appreciate the full range of benefits in the business case, however, author and readers alike must understand and agree on the definition of several benefits-related terms. These are familiar terms, but they are generally used with less precision than the business case requires. To some people, for instance, "benefits" simply means good things and "costs" are bad things. Or to some, perhaps, "cost" means spending money and "benefit" means money coming in. For the business case, however, the terms benefit and cost are better defined with reference to *business objectives:*

Benefit: A result that contributes *towards* meeting a business objective
Cost: A result that works *against* meeting a business objective.

These definitions provide a practical basis for bringing non financial outcomes into the case. Most people would agree that organizations of all kinds have objectives, and that meeting business objectives has *value*. This principle is the foundation of the benefits rationale presented here. Several other definitions are crucial to appreciating the rationale, however.

Two commonly used terms that are definitely *not* recommended for business case use, by the way, are "soft benefits" and "hard benefits." There is no universally agreed definition for these terms, but they are often used, anyway, in misleading ways. "Soft benefit," for example, implies that benefit is either unlikely to appear or impossible to measure. Unfortunately the term is sometimes applied to benefits that include contributions towards such things as customer satisfaction, the organization's image, branding, safety, or reduced risk. When a benefit is designated "soft," it looses respect in the eyes of most people, and the timid business case author may omit it from the case altogether.

Also unfortunately, those same objectives are sometimes called "intangibles," probably because they can be difficult or impossible to measure in financial terms. Tangible, however, means *touchable*, not "financial." If an outcome is truly *in*tangible, there is nothing to touch, nothing to measure, and no evidence that it occurred. It is more helpful when the business case author and reader think in these terms:

Tangible Benefit (or Cost): A benefit (or cost) with an observable, measurable impact. The impact may be financial or non financial. The impact may be directly measurable, or it may inferred from indirect evidence.

Intangible Benefit (or Cost): A benefit (or cost) with no observable, measurable impact.

Truly intangible benefits and costs do not belong in a business case.

Finally, everyone involved with the case should know that when benefits address non financial objectives, there *may* be a difference between the benefit and the business objective. Understanding this difference is crucial for bringing some non financial benefits into the case.

To illustrate the issue, consider first a common *financial* objective: cost savings. An organization may target cost savings through, perhaps, reducing electricity costs for office lighting. A proposal may include several actions such as replacing incandescent bulbs with fluorescent bulbs, adding skylight windows, and installing automatic shut off switches. In any case, progress towards the objective *cost savings* is measured in terms of—no surprise—expected *cost savings*. Results of the action are benefits that can be measured as electricity cost savings. In brief, the tangible evidence for the benefit and progress toward the financial objective are measured the same way.

Initiatives addressing *non financial* objectives, however, sometimes add an extra complexity: benefit and objective may be measured differently.

Consider an initiative targeting a non financial objective: improved customer satisfaction. The objective is non financial because customer satisfaction is defined and measured first in non financial terms (even though improved customer satisfaction should ultimately bring financial gains to a profit making business). Customer satisfaction cannot be measured directly—it is a condition of the customer mind. However, it can be inferred reasonably from indirect tangible measures such as customer survey scores, numbers of complaints, repeat business rates, and other measures (more on tangible measures follows in the next section).

The initiative targeting customer satisfaction might propose actions in a service call center that should reduce average customer call waiting time from, say, three minutes to 15 seconds. Here, the benefit (reduced waiting time) is measured differently from the objective (customer satisfaction). The author's challenge is to argue convincingly that a reduction in customer waiting time should contribute to improved customer survey scores, reduced customer complaints, and a higher repeat business rate.

Making Objectives Tangible

The **Benefits Rationale** block builds a foundation for bringing benefits into the case first by showing how business objectives are made tangible. Then, in subsequent steps, the block sets targets for the objectives, discusses the value of reaching targets, and connects benefit outcomes with progress towards the objectives. Business objectives that should be included here are the objectives for actions outlined in the **Subject Statement** block from the **Introduction Section** (pp. 14-15).

Making financial objectives tangible is usually no problem. Proposals of all kinds may target financial objectives defined as

- Net cash flow
- Cost savings
- Avoided costs[2]
- Sales revenues
- Cost per transaction
- Funding
- Total capital costs
- Gross profits
- Operating profits
- Earnings per share

It may be easy or it may be difficult to estimate how much progress to expect towards these objectives under different scenarios, but either way there is no question about how to *measure* progress: with currency units ($, £, €, ¥, and so on). When targets for these objectives are known, the value of reaching the target is also clear and obvious.

Proposals may also target objectives that are non financial, which can be measured rather directly, and which can be valued easily in financial terms as well. Examples for this class of objective include:

---

2. The difference between avoided costs and cost savings sometimes confuses people. *Cost savings* are a reduction in spending that is already taking place. An *avoided cost* has to do with a cost that has not occurred yet, but very likely will occur under Business as Usual.

Consider a call center operation, for instance, where daily call volume is increasing at a high rate. Under Business as Usual, more service operators will have to be hired soon to handle the increased call volume. There is, however, a proposed solution to increase service operator call capacity through improved call handling software, better operator access to information, and additional operator training. If the business case author shows convincingly that the proposed actions eliminate the need for additional operators, the Proposal scenario will show *avoided* hiring costs and *avoided* salaries for the additional operators.

Avoided costs are handled mathematically just like cost savings (see Exhibits 3.1 and 3.2, pp. 25-26). In order for avoided costs to appear legitimately as business case benefits, however, the author must show convincingly that those costs really will appear under Business as Usual.

- Increased market share
- Improved employee productivity
- Reduced employee turnover rate
- Reduced product delivery time
- Reduced mean-time-between-failure of product components

Most people readily grant legitimacy to benefits that contribute towards objectives like these. The financial value of meeting these objectives may be estimated rather directly in terms of such things as cost reductions, increased output, and increased incoming revenues.

Many people, however, have an especially difficult time bringing another class of benefits into the business case, even when the business objectives in view are very important. Difficulties can appear when benefits contribute to non financial objectives that must be measured and valued indirectly. Objectives of this kind may have to do with improvements in such things as:

- Customer satisfaction
- Employee satisfaction / Employee morale
- The organization's image
- Product image
- Branding
- Quality of welfare services delivered
- Safety / Reduced risk
- Readiness (e.g., readiness of a military unit)

If these items describe existing, established goals or objectives for the organization, some tangible measures or evidence for them should already be known before the author begins the business case.[3] (It is not easy to see how objectives for which there are no known measures or evidence would serve any useful purpose). In the organization, these measures may be called key performance indicators (KPIs), key performance measures (KPMs), success indicators, balanced scorecard metrics, or something similar.

Customer satisfaction, as mentioned earlier, cannot be measured directly but it can be inferred reasonably from tangible measures such as customer survey scores, numbers of complaints, repeat business rates, and other evidence. Similarly, employee satisfaction may be inferred from tangible evidence such as employee survey scores, productivity measures, absenteeism, disciplinary actions, and employee turnover.

Exhibit 3.4 (next page) illustrates a situation typical in many government organizations, where the business case supports decisions on funding project approval, program launch, service operations, major acquisitions, and other actions. The Department of Transportation for the US state of Oregon puts a *mission statement* at the top of its hierarchy of objectives, as do most other government, military, educational, health care, religious, or non profit organizations.

---

3. Some people try to make a distinction between the concepts *goal* and *objective*. Those who do so usually view goals as broader, higher level, and less tangible targets, while objectives are more specific and more tangible outcomes to aim for. The position presented here, in *Business Case Essentials*, is that a distinction between goals and objectives is more confusing than helpful, and serves no useful purpose for the business case. Here the two terms will be used interchangeably.

Oregon Department of Transportation

Mission

To provide a safe, efficient transportation system that supports economic opportunity and livable communities for Oregonians.

Goals

1. Improve traffic safety in Oregon.
2. Move people and goods efficiently.
3. Improve Oregon's livability and economic prosperity.

Goal 1. Improve Traffic Safety in Oregon
Key Performance Indicators

- Traffic Fatalities
  Traffic fatalities per 100 million vehicles miles traveled.

- Traffic Injuries
  Traffic injuries per 100 million vehicles miles traveled.

- Safe Drivers
  Percent of drivers who drove safely by avoiding traffic violations and accidents during the prior three years.

- Impaired Driving-Related Traffic Fatalities
  Percent of fatal traffic accidents that involved alcohol.

- Use of Safety Belts
  Percent of all vehicle occupants using safety belts.

- Large Truck At-Fault Crashes
  Number of large truck at-fault crashes per million vehicle miles traveled.

- Rail Crossing Incidents
  Number of highway-railroad at-grade incidents.

- Derailment Incidents
  Number of train derailments caused by human, track, or equipment error.

- Travelers Feel Safe
  Percent of public satisfied with transportation safety.

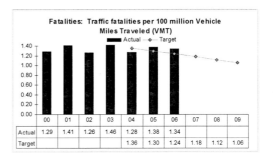

Fatalities: Traffic fatalities per 100 million Vehicle Miles Traveled (VMT)									
	00	01	02	03	04	05	06	07	08	09
Actual	1.29	1.41	1.26	1.46	1.28	1.38	1.34			
Target					1.36	1.30	1.24	1.18	1.12	1.06

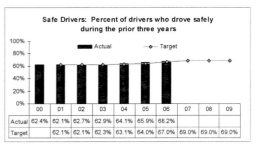

Safe Drivers: Percent of drivers who drove safely during the prior three years									
	00	01	02	03	04	05	06	07	08	09
Actual	62.4%	62.1%	62.7%	62.9%	64.1%	65.9%	68.2%			
Target		62.1%	62.1%	62.3%	63.1%	64.0%	67.0%	69.0%	69.0%	69.0%

64%, set in 2001, was chosen because existing data suggested that an increase of one-

From Oregon Department of Transportation Annual Performance Report Fiscal Year 2006-2007. Available at www.oregon.gov/ODOT/

Exhibit 3.4. Mission, Goals, and Key Performance Indicators for non financial objectives (from the US State of Oregon Department of Transportation). Progress towards a high level goal (improved traffic safety) is measured in tangible terms with nine key performance indicators (KPIs). Note that KPIs for goals 2 and 3 are not shown here. When the same KPIs are used consistently over time, targets can be set and performance tracked, as shown in the two examples at right.

Here, the mission is "To provide a safe, efficient transportation system that supports economic opportunities and livable communities ...." Mission statements like this would be nothing more than a vague expression of good intentions were they not translated into tangible, measurable terms.

In the Oregon example, the mission statement is first divided into three high level goals having to do with safety, economic opportunity, and livable communities. The exhibit also shows the nine key performance indicators (KPIs) defined as tangible measures for the goal

"Improved traffic safety." Safety can mean many things to different people, but in order to manage and evaluate the Department of Transportation progress towards that goal, safety is measured in very tangible terms such as the number of highway fatalities, or the percentage of "safe drivers" (drivers with no accidents or traffic violations in the last 3 years).

Targets for Objectives

Once the author names the business objectives addressed by a proposed action, and shows tangible measures for them, *targets* can be identified for each objective. Targets ultimately play a key role in establishing the value of both financial and non financial benefits. When a target is set, the author can ask "What is the value of reaching the target?" and then, "What is the value of the benefit that contributes towards reaching the target?" For non financial benefits and objectives, the "value" questions may or may not be answerable in financial terms.

In the Aerofirma example (from earlier chapters), the action proposals under consideration address objectives that are easily made tangible and assigned financial value. The Aerofirma **Subject Statement** presented several objectives for the proposed actions. The three top level objectives were:

1 Improve average gross margin per product and increase company gross profits for product sales.
2 Reduce design costs in change management.
3 Avoid hiring costs for additional design engineers, which would otherwise be needed over the next three years.

The **Benefits Rationale** block picks up where the Subject Statement left off, describing how these objectives translate into value for the organization. For each objective, the Benefits Rationale block describes how the objective is measured in tangible terms, sets a target for the objective, and describes the value of reaching the target. For these three objectives, the Benefits Rationale in the Aerofirma business case might state:

Business Objectives: Tangible Measures and Targets

1. Improve average gross margins and increase company gross profits for product sales.

Improvements in gross margin and gross profits will be addressed by meeting the following objectives:
- Enable higher levels of design customization for different customers, producing products which are sold at higher margins.
- Increase the number of products developed and sold each year, through improved design engineer productivity and reduced product development time.

Gross profits are net sales revenues less the direct costs of producing those revenues (Net Sales less Cost of Goods Sold). Gross margin is the gross profits expressed as a percentage of net sales revenues.

Product Gross Margin

The current Aerofirma Gross Margin is 47%. We believe this can be improved to 50.0% through design and sales of more complex higher margin mechanical assemblies. The higher levels of product complexity can only be achieved with the support of the proposed upgraded design system, as proposed in the "Proposed Upgrade" scenario and the "Combination Proposal" scenario.

Number of Product Designs/Year

Aerofirma currently completes and delivers an average of 40 design projects per year. Our target for the proposed actions is to increase the number of products developed and sold to an average of 45 per year. Engineering management affirms that this increase can be achieved either through (a) design engineer productivity improvements of about 10%, expected through the proposed design system software upgrade ("Upgrade" and "Combination" proposal scenarios), or (b) through increasing the number Aerofirma design engineering professionals by 10% ("Business as Usual Scenario").

Reaching both targets (gross margin improved from 47% to 50%, and product designs completed annually from 40 to 45) would improve annual Aerofirma gross profits from the current (2009) level of about $42,000,000 annually to about $44,000,000, an increase of about $2,000,000 annually.)

2. Reduce design costs for change management

Annual change management costs are significant engineering expenses, estimated for 2009 to reach $7,000,000. Engineering management estimates that upgrading from the two-dimensional design system to the proposed three-dimensional system can reduce change costs to about $2,000,000 annually, from two kinds of improvements in change management:

— First three-dimensional design should allow engineers to produce fewer "clashes" and other design problems that require change.

— Second, the proposed design system should enable engineers to identify a higher percentage of the necessary changes earlier in the design process (in the Concept Design and Detailed Design Phases), where change propagation is relatively faster and less expensive.

3 Avoid hiring costs for additional design engineers which would otherwise be needed over the next three years

Management has determined that engineering production must increase above the 2009 level by 10% for the years 2010 – 2012. This increase will either be achieved through hiring more design engineers ("Business as Usual" scenario) or through productivity gains with the proposed design software system upgrade ("Upgrade" and "Combination" proposal scenarios).

With current (2009) engineering labor and support costs at $23,400,000 a 10% increase in 2010 would be an an annual increment of $2,340,000, increasing by about 5% per year thereafter. This would be credited as an avoided cost benefit in under the proposal scenarios.

Here, the targets should be viewed as opportunities rather than expected outcomes. The different scenarios will very likely differ with respect to expected progress towards the targets. Different scenarios, that is, may anticipate different levels of benefits from addressing these objectives.

The Benefits Rationale block plays the same role when a proposed action targets non financial objectives. Referring the Oregon Department of Transportation example (Exhibit 3.4, p. 32), consider a proposed two-year initiative meant to improve safety at rail crossings and intersections that have a high accident rate. The initiative might propose actions such as road widening and grading, improved signage, and additional stoplights, signal lights, and street lightning. It might also include added police presence during especially dangerous hours, heavy traffic, or bad weather situations.

All of these actions are expensive, and the likely two-year costs can be estimated readily. However, other departments will certainly compete for the same public funds with entirely different proposals of their own. The Governor, the state Budget Office, and the state legislature, will naturally ask: Is funding this initiative a good business decision for the state? Or, should the funds be invested elsewhere?[5]

The business case can address these questions by showing how the cost of this initiative compares to the value returned—whether "value" is measured in financial terms or not. Here, it is reasonable to expect the initiative to impact several of the key performance indicators for safety, such as traffic fatalities, traffic injuries, rail crossing incidents, and perhaps others. The state has set targets for each indicator (Exhibit 3.4 has two examples), and it is not likely that any of the statewide targets will be reached through this initiative alone. However, the author can analyze existing data on accident rates and causes, and traffic flow patterns, and estimate reasonably how much progress towards each target to expect from this initiative.

Financial Value for Non Financial Objectives

When the case assigns no financial value to a target, benefits that contribute towards reaching the target contribute exactly "0" to the financial analysis. For that reason, the author and those who use the case for decision support and planning, should attempt to agree on a figure that represents the financial value of reaching objective targets—even for non financial objectives. The word "agree" is important here because the assigned value may include a subjective or arbitrary component.

There is no "one size fits all" approach for finding the appropriate financial value for a non financial target. Different objectives call for different approaches and the best we can do here is present several that work well in many situations[6].

---

5. In the real world, of course, decisions in government and in private industry are often based on political reasons, intuition, biases, loyalties, and other factors beyond the business case. This reality is not necessarily bad, as long as management objectives, priorities, and decision criteria are open and known.

6. For more examples and in-depth coverage on finding financial value for non financial targets, see *Getting Your Budget Approved* or *The Business Case Guide*. Information on these books is available at www.solutionmatrix.com.

- **Ask: Does reaching the target have direct or indirect consequences that do have financial value?**
  – An increase in market share should bring increased sales revenues.
  – An increase in employee productivity should result in greater output or lower operating expenses.
  – An improvement in customer satisfaction may translate into increased repeat business, greater customer retention rates, increased referral business, fewer customer complaints to handle, or lower costs of customer service operations.

- **Ask: What is the cost of not reaching the target?**
  – Not meeting mandatory emissions standards brings fines and other penalties.
  – Not fixing a product quality problem may result in lost sales and higher warranty expenses.
  – Not improving employee morale or employee satisfaction may result in lower productivity and higher employee turnover (bringing increased recruiting and hiring costs and new employee training costs).
  – Not improving the company image (or product image) may result in lost sales, lower market share, inability to price optimally, higher employee turnover, or inability to recruit high quality employees.

- **Ask: What is the next least costly means of achieving the same target result?**
  – A costly safety program targets a 50% reduction in the factory floor accident rate. Another way to achieve the same accident rate reduction would be to reduce production by 50% (which would have a known cost).

- **Ask: How does the objective target compare in importance with targets for other objectives that do have a known financial value?**
  – Again, a costly safety program targets a 50% reduction in the factory floor accident rate. Management agrees that reaching this target is as important or more important than reaching a targeted 10% increase in gross profits (which has a known financial value).

- **Ask: How much would management spend in order to reach the target?**
  – Management decides to spend $1M on initiatives that should result in industry leading customer satisfaction.

Some people may uneasy at first, using questions like these to assign financial value for a non financial target, probably because they seem to involve a subjective component (especially the last question). The business case author may have to help decision makers and other readers understand (preferably before the business case report is delivered) that it is perfectly reasonable to ask "'What is the value of reaching our targets? Managers, in fact, could not manage without a good sense for the value of reaching different objectives. Otherwise they could not direct the use of resources or prioritize proposals.

Finally, however, the author may have to conclude that a non financial objective cannot be assigned financial value in a way that is acceptable to everyone involved with the case. The author's task in the **Benefits Rationale** Block, then is to demonstrate in one way or another that an objective and its target are *important*. Again, here are some questions to ask that may support the idea that reaching the target is important:

- Ask: Is there a already an established target for the objective? Is the target highlighted in strategic plans, the organization's business plan, product plans, marketing plan, or any other important plan?,
- Ask: Has management supported previous projects, programs, or initiatives to pursue this objective?
- Ask: Are there budgeted funds for pursuing this objective?
- Ask: Is anyone's performance review based on progress toward this objective? Are projects, programs, or organizations evaluated with respect to progress on meeting this objective?
- Ask: Does this objective clearly support other important objectives?

If the answer to one or more of the above questions is "yes" there is a basis for showing that reaching the target is important, even if the basis is non financial. If the answers to each of the above is "No," the objective is not a good candidate for business case benefits.

Assumptions

Understanding the role of assumptions in the case is crucial for author and audience alike. A good business case will include an **Assumptions** block in the **Methods Section**, describing a few of the most important assumptions—those that are most helpful for understanding the case results. The many dozens or hundreds of other assumptions underlying the case can be described and explained in an appendix to the case report.

Major Assumptions

The **Assumptions** block for the **Methods Section** of the Aerofirma example case, for instance, might look like this:

Major Assumptions

Major assumptions underlying cost and benefit projections in this case include the following:

Under the Proposed Upgrade and Combination Proposal scenarios:

- The number of engineering change orders per year can be reduced by 75%, while the majority of remaining changes can be moved into the first two design process changes.
- Aerofirma market share can be increased 10% by the end of 2010, and increased another 5% per year after that.
- Market size for Aerofirma products will increase 5% by the end of 2010 and another 5% each year after that.

- In order to implement and fully benefit from new design capabilities, Aerofirma will need to invest about $200,000 in systems integration and other software consulting fees over the 3-year analysis period.
- Under the Combination Proposal scenario, Aerofirma will need to invest about $250,000 in management consulting fees over the 3-year analysis period.
- Design Engineers will complete training and reach full productivity improvements of 10% by the end of 2010.

How does the author know, by the way, that these six assumptions are the most important? A typical case, after all may include hundreds of assumptions. In order to know which are most important, the author performs a sensitivity analysis after building the financial model, and after making cost and benefit estimates for each scenario (See the **Sensitivity and Risk Analysis Section**, pp. 73-89). When the author has progressed that far, he or she can return to the **Methods Section** in the report and let readers know which assumptions will have the greatest impact on predicted outcomes.

Are Assumptions Necessary?

The business case, in fact, *must* stand on assumptions for at least three reasons:

- **First, the case predicts the future.**

Strictly speaking, everything we think we know about the future is an assumption, meaning that it comes with some uncertainty.

- **Second, the author has choices to make in designing scenarios.**

Think of the business case scenario as a detailed sketch of one way the future might work out. The future, however, can work out an infinite number of ways, and the author cannot sketch all of them. Instead, the author chooses specific outcomes to describe. In the Aerofirma Upgrade Proposal scenario, for instance, the author describes a future where software and hardware implementation are completed in one month starting mid January 2010. The month could start instead at any other time, or the author could have chosen a slower, phased implementation over a longer time period. But one month starting mid January is what the author assumed.

- **Third, assumptions simplify cost and benefit estimates.**

Salaries of the 40 Aerofirma design engineers over a three year time period will contribute to estimated cost and benefit figures. If the author knows with near certainty who these engineers are, and what their current salaries are now and will be over the next three years, there would be little need for an assumption. More likely, however, the author will simplify the estimate of future salary costs by assuming which job levels are involved, the average salary at each level, average pay increases to come, and so on.

Keeping Assumptions and Explanations in View

Assumptions play a critical role in explaining business case results, in building credibility for the case, and in measuring and reducing uncertainty for projections. Case builder and case recipients will return over and over to the assumptions behind the case, during and after the case building project. The problem, however, is that a typical case may very well rest on hundreds of different assumptions, far too many to hold reliably in human memory. It is vitally important, therefore, that case builders record assumptions *as they are made*. It is just as important to record the reasons for making the specific assumption.

Consider, for instance, the Aerofirma assumption that design engineers will reach full proficiency on the new system by the end of 2010. This date is important for business case results, because it helps determine the point in time when benefits from the new design system reach their target values (e.g., in increased productivity, fewer design errors, or ability to complete more complex designs). The author will want to record the assumption and, in an appendix to the report, document the reasons for making that assumption. For example:

Assumption:

- Design Engineers will complete training and reach full productivity improvements of 10% by the end of 2010.

The assumption is based on these factors:

- The vendor reports that experienced design engineers typically require two full weeks of formal instruction to make the transition from two-dimensional design to three-dimensional design systems.
- We assume that design engineer training will begin mid January 2010.
- 7-14 days of initial training will be spread across a one month period, to allow engineers to maintain progress on work in progress during the training period.
- The vendor also reports that design engineers typically require about six to 10 months post-training experience working with real design projects in order to reach full proficiency.

Scope and Boundaries

Whose costs belong in the case? Whose benefits belong in the case? For what future time period will they be estimated? For most cases, the answers are not automatically determined by stating the subject and purpose of the business case. Often there is some room for differences of opinion and arbitrary judgement. Different analysts may take the same subject and purpose and return with quite different business case results if they answer differently to the above questions, and both cases may be legitimate or "correct."

The questions need to be answered at the start of the case-building project and stated clearly in the business case report, preferably in a **Scope and Boundaries** block in the **Methods Section.** The answers are necessary for building the cost model (next block) and for assigning value to benefits (established in the previous block, the **Benefits Rationale).**

Scope is the range of coverage encompassed by the case along several dimensions. Boundaries define the scope precisely, providing rules for deciding which data fall within the scope and of the case and which do not.

One dimension that always needs bounding is:

Time

- When does the analysis period begin, and when does it end?
- Is the analysis synchronized with calendar years? Fiscal years? Project or program plans?

Other dimensions that *may* need bounding include:

Geography/Location

- Are the costs borne by a specific site? Are the benefits recognized by a specific site? Or, does the whole company/organization gain from the benefits. Do the costs (or the benefits) represent a fictional but "typical" site? Multiple sites?
- Do the costs cover specific areas only? (E.g., a manufacturing floor, computer room, loading dock, executive offices)

Organization or Function

- Will the costs be paid from the budget of a specific division, department or group? Or, the whole company or organization?
- Do the costs or the benefits apply only to certain functions? (E.g., manufacturing, marketing, sales, etc.)
- Do the costs or the benefits apply to certain personnel but not others? (E.g., hourly-paid labor, management, IT/IS staff but not computer users, union employees only, etc.)

Technology

- Does the analysis cover computer hardware but not software?
- Vehicle engine and drive train maintenance, but not body work?
- Electrical but not mechanical devices?

Scope and boundary statements tell case developers and readers just whose costs and benefits are included—and the ownership of costs may very well be different from the ownership of benefits. It is common, for instance, for one department (e.g., Information Technology) to cover the costs from its budget, but for the benefits to be realized company wide. Or, in a government business case, the costs are covered from the organization budget, but the benefits may be credited to the entire population served by the organization.

Whose costs belong in the case? Whose benefits belong in the case? For what future time period will they be estimated? The Aerofirma example case might address these questions with a **Scope and Boundaries** block that looks like the following. The first paragraph repeats the lead sentence in "naming the action" from the subject statement.

This case examines the likely 3-year costs and benefits to Aerofirma Corporation from several proposed changes within design engineering and manufacturing, intended to reduce costs, improve design abilities, and shorten design and manufacturing times.

- **Analysis Period**
  Costs and benefits will be assessed for several action scenarios covering a three-year analysis period, beginning 1 January 2010 and ending 31 December 2012.

- **Costs**
  - Capital costs will be borne by the Aerofirma corporate capital budgets for 2010-2012.
  - Professional labor costs and other engineering and manufacturing expenses will be will be provided by the Engineering and Manufacturing Departmental operating budgets for 2010-2012.
  - Human Resources management and training costs will be provided by the Aerofirma Corporate Human Resources operating budgets for the analysis period.
  - Contract labor for system installation and integration, and professional consulting services for process analysis and organizational development will be covered by the Aerofirma Corporate Research and Development budgets for 2010-2012.
  - General management time will be covered by the Aerofirma SG&A operating budgets for the analysis period time.

- **Benefits**
  - Benefits in the form of increased sales revenues and gross profits will be recognized by the entire company
  - Benefits in the form of reduced change costs and avoided engineering hiring costs will be realized in Engineering operating budgets, benefitting the company's reported income statement performance.

Now we know which budget categories will provide funds over the analysis period (whose costs are involved) and where the financial benefits will be recognized (benefits will accrue to the whole company). Since Aerofirma has only one site, there is no need to indicate define scope and boundaries for location

Incidentally, Aerofirma is a design and manufacturing company in private industry, but were Aerofirma a government or non profit organization, the scope of the benefits coverage would probably have been much wider. As mentioned, these organizations are usually mandated to consider value to the populations served.

Cost Model

How do you know that every important cost and benefit item is included in the case? How do you know that different scenarios are truly comparable? A clear presentation of the **benefits rationale** (pp. 28-37) and a **cost model** (this block) provides the means for assuring everyone that the case includes all relevant line items and only relevant line items. By applying a single cost model and benefits rationale to all scenarios, the author can assure everyone that data selection was unbiased, and complete, and that different scenarios were compared fairly.

The term "cost model" as used here is not an exercise in advanced or complex cost accounting. On the contrary, it's virtue and power lie in its simplicity and clarity. The model presented here is simply a system for identifying and naming cost categories. The model design is successful if it conveys *self-evident completeness*. This means that author and audience alike should be able to review the cost categories for the model and agree with confidence that the model as a whole holds all costs that belong in the case and only those costs.

The author can begin designing and building the cost model for the case once the following are known:

- The number of scenarios in the case and the major actions proposed for each from the subject statement (see pp. 13-17).
- The financial metrics, or decision criteria, that decision makers and planners are looking for in the case from the purpose statement (see pp. 24-27).
- The scope and boundaries of the case (whose costs and whose benefits will be estimated over which time period, see pp. 39-41)

Two Approaches to Cost Modeling

Two approaches to cost modeling are illustrated here:

- The resource based cost model.
- The activity based cost model.

The two approaches are very similar, and in principle, either approach should lead the author to the same set of cost items and cash flow figures. In reality, however, one approach is a more natural fit (easier to work with) for some business case subjects, while the other is a better fit for other subjects. The resource-based approach is often chosen when the case is primarily about the acquisition of assets, where the assets have an expected useful life, and where they bring ongoing operating costs and maintenance costs. Cases about the acquisition of major IT systems, vehicles, factory machinery, buildings, or expensive laboratory equipment, for example, are usually good subjects for this approach.

On the other hand, the activity-based approach is usually a better approach to cost analysis when the proposed actions under study are essentially a project, program, or service delivery, where the costs are primarily human labor.

Finally, many business case subjects are best approached with a hybrid model, using an activity based approach for some cost categories and a resource based approach for others.

The Resource Based Cost Model

In the resource based approach the analyst takes the question "Where do costs come from?" and answers: "Costs come from using resources." The matrix in Exhibit 3.5 (next page) and Exhibit 3.6 (p.44) is a resource based cost model that works well for many IT-related business case studies—such as Aerofirma's analysis of a proposed design system upgrade. This model

Exhibit 3.5 A resource based cost model example where the business case subject is a proposed IT system acquisition. Individual cells are populated with cost items, described as named resources. The full model is shown with cost items in Exhibit 3.6, next page.

Resources	IT System Life Cycle Categories		
	Acquisition	Operations	Change
Hardware			
Software			
Personnel			
NW & Comm			
Facilities			

includes every cost impact item that follows from both proposal scenarios, as well as it costs expected under business as usual. It is a *resource based* model because

- One axis of the model represents resource categories (the vertical axis)
- Individual cost items are identified as named resources (see Exhibit 3.6).

The cost model is really just an organized list of cost items. Potential cost items are grouped into into cells: each cell holds a group of cost items that may change together and which need to be planned and managed together (often because they have common cost drivers). The upper left cell, for instance, holds all "Hardware Acquisition Costs." Each cell in fact can have a long list of cost items.

Notice also that the cost universe is divided in two ways. The horizontal dimension groups cost items by "IT System Life Cycle" categories (Acquisition, Operation, and Change). Every IT cost item in the case fits into one of these categories. The scheme makes sense, because acquisition costs are planned and managed differently from continuing operational costs and growth and change costs. The design of this axis is successful if the author and audience can agree that these columns include *all* of the life cycle event categories that belong in the case.

The vertical dimension divides all costs into five different "Resource" categories: Hardware, Software, Personnel, Networking and Communications, and Facilities costs (the more detailed example in Exhibit 3.6 has the Personnel resource category further divided into sections, "IT Staff Costs" and "User Costs"). The vertical axis scheme also makes sense, because each resource category is planned and managed differently from the others. And, the vertical axis design is successful if author and audience agree that the categories on this axis cover *all* the resource categories that belong in the case.

Organizing cost items by categories in this way creates a surprisingly powerful tool for identifying, analyzing, and communicating the "cost" side of the business case. With a cost model, case builders and case recipients have a simple, visual rule that show which cost items belong in the case. If a cost item does not fit in one of the cells, the item does not belong in the case. When there are two or more scenarios in the case, we ensure comparability of scenarios by using the same cost model for all scenarios. Individual scenarios may turn up different line items within cells, but the scenario costs are comparable because all scenarios are analyzed with the same cost model structure.

IT System Life Cycle Categories

	Acquisition & Implementation Costs *Costs at acquisition or during initial implementation*	Operation Costs *Periodic or frequently occurring costs that continue 3 years.*	Ongoing Change & Growth Costs *These costs come with adds, moves and changes to the computing environment*
Hardware Costs	• Server system purchase or upgrade • PC system purchase • Engineering WS system purchase • Storage space purchase • Other peripheral HW	• HW maintenance fees • HW lease expenses	• Additional server systems • Additional client systems • Additional server CPUs • System upgrades • Storage space expansion • Other peripheral HW
Software Costs	Operating System (OS) original purchase/license • Application purchase, one-time charge • Development/migration SW purchase	• Periodic SW license fees • SW maintenance/warranty fees	• OS upgrade • Migration software purchase

Personnel Costs: IT Staff	• Preplanning costs
	In-house or outside consultant
	• HW Installation labor
	• SW Installation labor OS, *OS utilities, appl ications*
	  – Install at Server
	  – Install at client
	• Initial NW set up
	  – Set up user accounts
	  – Directory creation labor
	  – Set up /install NW services
	  – Set up/install NW or mail server
	• SW migration labor
	• Initial training costs (professionals)
	• Professional hiring costs
		• Administrative labor
		  – Systems operators
		  – Systems programmers
		  – Applications programmers
		  – Network admin labor
		  – Storage management
		  – IT/IS management
		  – Other Admin
		• Trouble shooting
		• Continuing contract labor
		• Continuing training (professional)
			• HW reconfiguring, setup
			• OS upgrade labor
			  – Upgrade at server
			  – Upgrade at client
			• NW changes -Administrative costs
			  – Add/move/delete user accounts
			  – Add/move/delete a NW service
			  – Add/change a NW or mail server
			  – Assign/change security
			• Capacity planning, other change planning (in-house)
			• Capacity planning, other change planning/consulting (outside source)
			• Temporary contract labor
			• General moving labor

Personnel Costs: Users	• Initial training costs (users) • Organizational downtime costs during install or upgrade	• User Trouble shooting, system management • User help / other user services • Continuing training (users)	• Additional user training
NW & Comms	• NW/Comms HW (including NW server systems • NW/comm SW • Line acquisition/hookup charges • Installation of comm wiring, cables	• Line usage charges • Satellite or other WAN charges • Wireless charges • Outside internet service providers	• NW change planning costs • Additional NW/comm HW and SW • Additional cables, site/preparation for changes
Facilities Costs	• Floor space acquisition, renovation, construction • Initial site planning	• Electricity • Security costs (e.g. disaster recovery services)	• Site expansion • Site consolidation, • Site renovation

*(left margin label: **Resources**)*

Exhibit 3.6 The full resource-based cost model from Exhibit 3.5. Individual cell entries are cost items that appear with cash flow estimates on the business case cash flow statements.

The Activity Based Cost Model

When human labor accounts for most of the resource costs in the analysis, an activity based approach to cost modeling may be preferred. With this approach, the author takes the question "Where do costs come from?" and answers: "Costs come from *activities*." Building the cost model becomes an exercise in anticipating whose labor is going to be involved, and which activities they will perform.

Exhibit 3.7 (next page), for instance is an activity based model for a business case about a new product proposal. Here, unlike the resource based example in Exhibits 3.5 and 3.6, this model's horizontal axis *does* represent a time line: There is a prescribed sequence to project phase, product life cycle phases, or program phases, and their transition points can be tied to calendar dates. Each column is a list of what is done in each phase. The horizontal axis design is successful if author and audience agree that it covers all cost-causing activities that belong in the case, and if the phase names are helpful in identifying who does what, and when.

The vertical axis categories in this model are essentially *people* categories. In this case, Sales, Marketing, and Engineering, for instance could be the names of organizations or job functions. Here, the axis design is successful if author and audience agree that the categories capture all activities that will belong in the case, and (as with the horizontal axis) these categories are helpful in determining who does what, and when. Organizing a cost model this way, incidentally, makes it easy to tie the proposal to operating budgets for different organizations (vertical axis) across different planning periods (horizontal axis).

Which Approach: Resource or Activity Based Model?

When it is time to project cash flow figures for individual cost items, the author must predict *resource needs,* regardless of which kind of cost model is used. The usual calculation for labor costs, for instance, multiplies a number of labor units times the cost per unit (30 person days x $200/day = $6,000, for instance). The labor requirement in hours, days, or person years is required whether the labor cost item is described as an activity ("Identify market material needs") or as a resource (Systems operators labor). Just *how* the author decides to make that resource estimate plays a role in deciding between cost modeling approaches.

The resource based model example in Exhibit 3.6, for example, identifies one cost item as "Administrative labor–Systems operators." (Under Personnel Costs / Operation Costs). The model says nothing about the activities these people perform. In this case, the business case author might simply agree with the IT manager, that systems operator requirements over the 3-year analysis period might be 2 FTE (full time equivalent persons per year). Estimates like this might draw upon their experience with similar implementations, information from the vendor, advice from consultants, or other sources. Here the labor requirement can be scoped without analyzing who will do which tasks or when.

On the other hand, the activity based model in Exhibit 3.7 identifies a cost item for Service personnel labor to "Deliver service technician training," and in the same cell, another item is Service personnel labor to "Produce service manuals and online documentation." Here, the author and Service Manger know that in under to estimate the number of trainer hours, or tech-

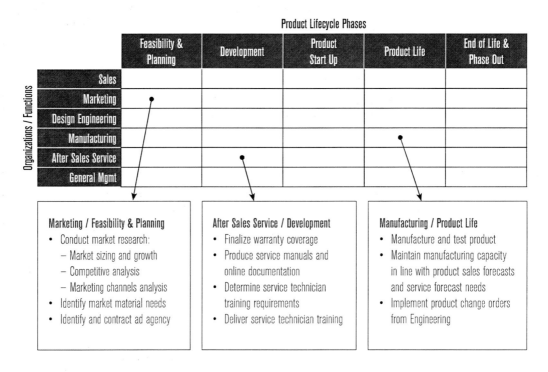

Exhibit 3.7. An **activity based** cost model example where the business case subject is the proposed development and launch of a new product offering. Cost items for in each cell are activities (cost items for 3 of the model's 30 cells are illustrated).

nical writer hours required, they must identify specific tasks. Here, none of these people will be assigned full time to these tasks—indeed each of them are working simultaneously to support several initiatives or projects and the best way to estimate how much their time goes specifically into the business case subject is to think in terms of specific activities. The activity based model is especially well suited to cases where the author can draw upon an existing project plan or work breakdown structure, or where the organization already uses "activity based costing."

Cost Items for Cash Flow Statements

Cost items on the business case cash flow statements for each scenario come from the cost model. Here, in Exhibit 3.8 (next page, upper) is the cost model for the Aerofirma example case as it appears in the business case report, while Exhibit 3.9 (next page, lower) shows how the model's cost items appear in each full value cash flow statement Cash flow statements themselves appear in the next major section of the report, **Business Results**.

Business Case Cost Model

		ACQUISITION & CHANGE System Acquisition, Migration, Upgrade & Deployment Costs	OPERATIONS Continuing Operating Costs
RESOURCES	Software	• One-time license - Design SW • One-time license - Database SW • One-time license - Admin SW	• SW Maintenance costs
	Hardware	• Server systems purchase/upgrade • Desktop systems purchase/upgrade • NW/Comm HW purchase/upgrade	• Server systems maintenance • Desktop systems maintenance • NW/Comm maintenance
	Engineering Design & Mfg Labor	• Initial training - Design engineers • Initial training - Manufacturing mgmt	• Design engineering labor • Manufacturing labor • Change costs / Change management
	IT Support Personnel	• Initial training - IT support • SW install & migration labor (internal)	• Continuing training - IT support • SW and HW operations labor • User Help Desk
	External Services	• SW install & migration servces • Process analysis & mgmt consulting	• Systems integration services

Exhibit 3.8 Business Case Cost Model for the Aerofirma Example case, as presented in the business case report. The same model is applied to all scenarios in the case.

Exhibit 3.9. The line items from the cost model appear in each scenario cash flow statement. The Costs section of one scenario statement is shown here. All scenarios have the same structure and line items, but the estimated figures will very likely differ among scenarios.

COSTS Cash outflows	Yr 0 31 Dec 2009	Yr 1 31 Dec 2010	Yr 2 31 Dec 2011	Yr 3 31 Dec 2012	TOTAL
Software					
One-time license - Design SW.....................$	~~~	~~~	~~~	~~~	~~~
One-time license - Database SW.................$	~~~	~~~	~~~	~~~	~~~
One-time license - Admin software...............$	~~~	~~~	~~~	~~~	~~~
Annual software maintenance.......................$	~~~	~~~	~~~	~~~	~~~
Total Software	$ ~~~	~~~	~~~	~~~	~~~
Hardware					
Server system purchase/upgrade..................$	~~~	~~~	~~~	~~~	~~~
Desktop system purchase/upgrade ..$	~~~	~~~	~~~	~~~	~~~
NW & Comm hardware purchase/upgrade......$	~~~	~~~	~~~	~~~	~~~
Server system HW maintenance...................$	~~~	~~~	~~~	~~~	~~~
Desktop system HW maintenance.................$	~~~	~~~	~~~	~~~	~~~
NW & Comm HW maintenance......................$	~~~	~~~	~~~	~~~	~~~
Total Hardware	$ ~~~	~~~	~~~	~~~	~~~
Engineering Design & Mfg Labor					
Intial training - Design engineers..................$	~~~	~~~	~~~	~~~	~~~
Initial training - Manufacturing management....$	~~~	~~~	~~~	~~~	~~~
Design engineering labor............................$	~~~	~~~	~~~	~~~	~~~
Manufacturing labor....................................$	~~~	~~~	~~~	~~~	~~~
Change costs / Change management...........$	~~~	~~~	~~~	~~~	~~~
Total Engineering Design & Mfg Labor	$ ~~~	~~~	~~~	~~~	~~~
IT Support Personnel					
Initial training - IT support..........................$	~~~	~~~	~~~	~~~	~~~
Installation & migration labor, internal.............$	~~~	~~~	~~~	~~~	~~~
Continuing training - IT support....................$	~~~	~~~	~~~	~~~	~~~
SW and HW operations labor.......................$	~~~	~~~	~~~	~~~	~~~
User help desk..$	~~~	~~~	~~~	~~~	~~~
Total Support Personnel	$ ~~~	~~~	~~~	~~~	~~~
External Services					
SW installation and migration services.......... ..$	~~~	~~~	~~~	~~~	~~~
Systems integration services.......................$	~~~	~~~	~~~	~~~	~~~
Process analysis & mgmt consulting..............$	~~~	~~~	~~~	~~~	~~~
Total External Services	$ ~~~	~~~	~~~	~~~	~~~
Total Costs	$ ~~~	~~~	~~~	~~~	~~~

You may recognize the Aerofirma model as a simpler variation of the resource based model in Exhibit 3.6. Here, the author and audience have agreed that these 10 categories and 23 cost items cover all relevant costs in all scenarios. On the cash flow statement extract (Exhibit 3.9) you should also see that the Resource axis from the cost model has carried over into the cash flow statement. In the cash flow statement, however, the horizontal axis is replaced with columns representing years in the analysis period.

Data Sources

The cost model and benefits rationale identify and organize cost/benefit line items. Scope and boundary statements determine where they are measured. These design elements for the case should be presented in the **Methods Section** of the business case report, as described above.

Those who read the report also need to know to know how cost and benefit values are measured, or where they come from. Some of this understanding comes from the author's presentation of assumptions underlying the case: Major assumptions appear in the **Assumptions block** (pp. 37-38) in the **Methods Section**, and other assumptions are collected in the report appendix.

Many of the author's assumptions, however, will be based on data or information from a variety of sources. A **Data Sources** block in this section adds credibility to the case by identifying these sources. Since many of the sources, are updated or otherwise change over time, case readers will need to know the date or version of the source used for the current business case..

Some sources that might be named in this block could include such things as:

- The organization's business plan.
- Budgets: operating budgets, capital budgets (historical, current, or future).
- Spending records or other historical information.
- Experience from similar projects or proposals.
- IT capacity planning / resource planning analyses.
- Vendor proposals.
- Feasibility studies.
- Pilot projects.
- Outside consultant's estimates.
- Published industry averages, benchmarks, or "best-in-class" figures.

Chapter 3 Summary

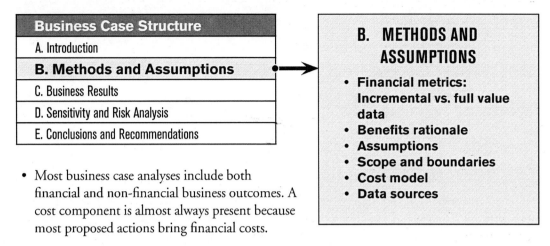

- Most business case analyses include both financial and non-financial business outcomes. A cost component is almost always present because most proposed actions bring financial costs.

- Financial costs enter the case as cash outflows and financial benefits enter as cash inflows.

- A Financial Metrics block illustrates the structure of the financial model, the kinds of cash flow data analyzed, and the financial metrics to be developed from cash flow figures.

- Cost savings and avoided costs are measured by comparing cash outflows in a proposal scenario to cash outflows for the same items in a baseline (Business as Usual) scenario.

- A Benefits Rationale block serves to legitimize benefits for the case and show how their value is established.

- For the business case, a benefit is defined as a contribution towards meeting a business objective. A cost is defined as a result that works against meeting a business objective.

- For most benefits, the author must establish tangible measures for the benefit (outcome) and the business objective it contributes to. The author's task is to connect tangible outcomes with tangible measures for the objectives.

- The Methods Section should contain an Assumption block that identifies the most important assumptions underlying the cost and benefit estimates.

- Scope and Boundaries statements specify whose costs and whose benefits belong in the case, and the time period for which they will be estimated.

- The Methods Section should include a cost model, showing which cost categories and cost items belong in the case. A good cost model leaves no doubt that these categories cover all costs relevant to the case and only those costs.

- Cost items for the cost model may be defined as resources (in a resource-based model) or as activities (in an activity-based model).

- A Data Sources block in the Methods Section adds credibility by identifying the major sources of information for the case (e.g., vendor proposals or business plans).

Chapter 4

Business Results

Building blocks in this section are the case's reason for being. The case exists, after all, to answer questions such as: "What would the financial consequences be if we take the proposed action?" "What are the important non financial outcomes? Here is where these questions are answered concretely. Data summaries and analyses should be presented objectively and directly, keeping interpretations and explanatory text to a minimum.

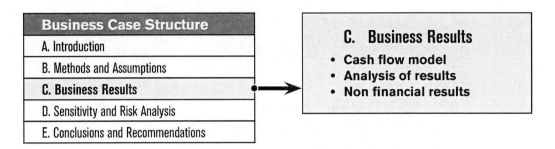

Business Case Structure
A. Introduction
B. Methods and Assumptions
C. Business Results
D. Sensitivity and Risk Analysis
E. Conclusions and Recommendations

C. Business Results
- **Cash flow model**
- **Analysis of results**
- **Non financial results**

In the business case **Introduction Section**, the author identifies one or more scenarios for evaluation. The rest of the case addresses questions such as these: "What happens if we implement each scenario? Which scenario represents the recommended course of action?" The "What happens?" question will be answered here in the **Business Results Section**, in *business terms*—financial and non financial business results. The recommendation will come later, in the **Conclusions and Recommendations Section**, based on further analysis and scenario comparisons.

Cash Flow Model

Financial results under each scenario appear in a **Cash Flow Model**. In the business case report this model includes a set of cash flow statements—one full value statement for each scenario, as well as incremental cash flow statements (as introduced in the **Financial Metrics** block, pp. 24-27). The complete cash flow model shows how expected costs and benefits work together to produce cash flow results for each scenario, and how the scenarios compare with each other..

In a simple business case with just one scenario, the cash flow model may be nothing more than a single cash flow statement representing a proposed action scenario. If the case purpose is decision support, there will be a full value cash flow statement for each decision option in view. Insofar as possible, the author will also want to include a baseline scenario, that is a "Business as Usual" (BAU) scenario, so as enable the measurement of *differences* that show up as savings, improvements, increases, or decreases. These differences appear in the incremental cash flow statements.

Exhibit 4.1 (next page) represents the set of cash flow statements appropriate for the Aero-firma example case, while Exhibits 4.2, 4.3, and 4.4 (pp. 54-56) show how three of the five cash flow statements actually appear.

These examples predict future cash flows. If you have training in financial accounting, you may wish to compare these examples with the standard form historical cash flow report, often called the "Statement of Changes in Financial Position," The business case cash flow statements are very similar to the financial accounting report with just a few important differences. Notice that:

- Cash inflows on the financial accounting report come under the major heading "Sources of Cash." Cash inflows on the business case cash flow statement come under "Benefits."
- The financial accounting report lists cash outflows under the major heading "Uses of Cash." In the business case cash flow statement, the heading for cash outflows is "Costs."
- Financial accounting cash flow reports are historical reports, looking backwards in time across the previous quarter, year, or several years. The business case cash flow statements look forward in time.

Otherwise the cash flow statement in the business case is just like other cash flow reports: it includes only line items that represent true cash inflows or outflows. Depreciation expense, for example, appears on the income statement but not on cash flow reports because it is not a true cash outflow.

Negative and Positive Numbers

Notice also the convention here, of using positive numbers for projected cash inflows and nega-tive numbers for projected cash outflow. As explained in the **Financial Metrics** block (see pp. 24-27), this convention helps avoid confusion about which numbers are added or subtracted with each other, and it also makes it easy to compare fully value cash flow statements via the incremental cash flow statements, such as Exhibit 4.4.

Cost Savings and Avoided Costs as Benefits

In the Aerofirma case, there is only one benefit item on the Proposed Upgrade scenario full value cash flow statement. That benefit is "Gross Profits–Product Sales" (Exhibit 4.2). Notice, however, that the incremental cash flow statement for the same scenario (Exhibit 4.4) has *three* benefit items: (1) "Gross Profits–Product Sales," (2) "Avoided costs–Design engineering Labor" and (3) "Savings–Change Costs/Management."

The two cost items had lower values in the Proposal scenario than in Business as Usual, creating projected cash inflows in the incremental cash flow statement. Projected cash inflows are benefits.

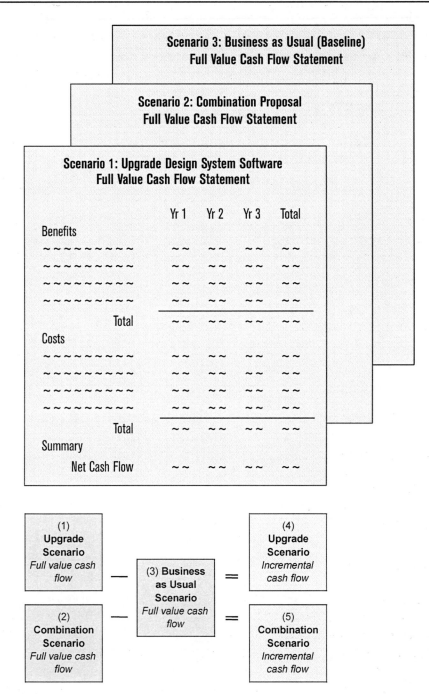

Exhibit 4.1. The cash flow model for the Aerofirma Example Case. Full value cash flow statements for each scenario (top) all have the same line items and structure. Both proposal scenario full value statements (1 and 2) are compared to the same Business as Usual cash flow statement (3) to produce incremental cash flow statements (4 and 5). Examples of three of the five statements are shown in Exhibits 4.2, 4.3, and 4.4, on following pages.

Full Value Cash Flow Statement: Proposed Upgrade Scenario

Net Cash Flow...............................$	97,343.3	*$ in 1000s*
Net Present Value (NPV) at 8.0% ....$	82,923.1	
Total Benefits/Gains.......................$	145,848.0	
Total Costs...................................$	(48,504.7)	
Analysis Period..............................	1-Jan-2010 through 31-Dec-2012	

$ in 1000s	Yr 0	Yr 1 31 Dec 2010	Yr 2 31 Dec 2011	Yr 3 31 Dec 2012	TOTAL
BENEFITS / GAINS (Cash inflows)					
Gross profits - Product sales ....$	0.0	44,978.0	48,520.0	52,350.0	145,848.0
Total Benefits/Gains $	0.0	44,978.0	48,520.0	52,350.0	145,848.0
COSTS (Cash outflows)					
Software					
One-time license - Design SW.............$	(149.4)	(125.0)	(126.7)	(88.3)	(489.3)
One-time license - Database SW..........$	(24.9)	(15.2)	(15.2)	(12.0)	(67.3)
One-time license - Admin SW..............$	(28.4)	(20.2)	(14.3)	(14.3)	(77.2)
Annual software maintenance..............$	0.0	(37.2)	(51.0)	(63.0)	(151.2)
Total Software $	(202.7)	(197.6)	(207.2)	(177.5)	(785.0)
Hardware					
Server system purchase/upgrade.........$	(185.0)	(42.0)	(42.0)	(35.0)	(304.0)
Desktop system purchase/upgrade ....$	(84.0)	(62.0)	(38.0)	(40.0)	(224.0)
NW & Comm HW purchase/UG..... ....$	(25.4)	(44.0)	(35.0)	(35.0)	(139.4)
Server system HW maintenance..........$	0.0	(22.7)	(26.9)	(30.4)	(80.0)
Desktop system HW maintenance........$	0.0	(14.6)	(18.4)	(22.4)	(55.4)
NW & Comm HW maintenance............$	0.0	(6.9)	(10.4)	(13.9)	(31.3)
Total Hardware $	(294.4)	(192.2)	(170.7)	(176.7)	(834.1)
Engineering Design& Mfg Labor					
Initial training - Design engineers..........$	108.0	(80.0)	(30.0)	(30.0)	(32.0)
Initial training - Manufacturing mgmt......$	(44.0)	(22.0)	0.0	0.0	(66.0)
Design engineering labor....................$	0.0	(5,109.0)	(5,211.2)	(5,315.4)	(15,635.6)
Manufacturing labor...........................$	0.0	(6,259.5)	(6,384.7)	(6,703.9)	(19,348.1)
Change costs / Change mgmt.............$	0.0	(4,280.8)	(2,810.6)	(1,830.5)	(8,921.9)
Total Engr Design & Mfg Labor $	64.0	(15,751.3)	(14,436.5)	(13,879.8)	(44,003.6)
IT Support Personnel					
Initial training - IT support..................$	(40.0)	0.0	0.0	0.0	(40.0)
Install & migration labor, internal..........$	0.0	(234.5)	(239.2)	(244.0)	(717.7)
Continuing training - IT support...........$	0.0	(66.0)	(66.0)	(66.0)	(198.0)
SW and HW operations labor..............$	0.0	(469.0)	(478.4)	(469.0)	(1,416.5)
User help desk................................$	0.0	(93.3)	(47.6)	(48.6)	(189.5)
Total IT Support Personnel $	(40.0)	(862.9)	(831.2)	(827.6)	(2,561.7)
External Services					
SW install & migration services............$	(48.5)	(35.0)	(35.0)	(20.0)	(138.5)
Systems integration services..............$	(25.7)	(22.0)	(22.0)	(22.0)	(91.7)
Process analysis & mgmt consult.........$	(30.0)	(20.0)	(20.0)	(20.0)	(90.0)
Total External Services $	(104.2)	(77.0)	(77.0)	(62.0)	(320.2)
Total Costs $	(577.3)	(17,081.0)	(15,722.6)	(15,123.7)	(48,504.7)
CASH FLOW SUMMARY (Cash inflows (outflows))					
Benefits..$	0.0	44,978.0	48,520.0	52,350.0	145,848.0
Costs..$	(577.3)	(17,081.0)	(15,722.6)	(15,123.7)	(48,504.7)
NET CASH FLOW ....$	**(577.3)**	**27,897.0**	**32,797.4**	**37,226.3**	**97,343.3**
Cumulative net cash flow ....$	(577.3)	27,319.6	60,117.0	97,343.3	
Discounted cash flow at 8.0% ....$	(577.3)	25,830.5	28,118.4	29,551.4	82,923.1

Exhibit 4.2 The full value cash flow statement for the Proposed Upgrade Scenario in the Aerofirma Example Case.

Full Value Cash Flow Statement: Business as Usual Scenario

Net Cash Flow..............................$ 76,787.6	$ in 1000s
Net Present Value (NPV) at 8.0% ....$ 65,593.1	
Total Benefits/Gains.......................$ 139,583.0	
Total Costs...................................$ (62,795.4)	
Analysis Period.............................. 1-Jan-2010 through 31-Dec-2012	

$ in 1000s	Yr 0	Yr 1 31 Dec 2010	Yr 2 31 Dec 2011	Yr 3 31 Dec 2012	TOTAL
BENEFITS / GAINS (Cash inflows)					
Gross profits - Product sales ....$	0.0	42,933.5	46,432.6	50,216.9	139,583.0
Total Benefits/Gains $	0.0	42,933.5	46,432.6	50,216.9	139,583.0
COSTS (Cash outflows)					
Software					
One-time license - Design SW.............$	(70.0)	(101.6)	(82.0)	(28.0)	(281.6)
One-time license - Database SW..........$	(18.0)	(15.3)	(15.3)	(8.4)	(57.0)
One-time license - Admin SW..............$	(20.2)	(15.2)	(8.5)	(8.5)	(52.3)
Annual software maintenance..............$	0.0	(26.9)	(36.2)	(39.9)	(103.1)
Total Software $	(108.2)	(159.0)	(141.9)	(84.8)	(493.9)
Hardware					
Server system purchase/upgrade.........$	(45.0)	(32.0)	(32.0)	(32.0)	(141.0)
Desktop system purchase/upgrade ....$	(56.0)	(44.0)	(39.0)	(39.0)	(178.0)
NW & Comm HW purchase/UG..... ....$	(25.4)	(44.0)	(35.0)	(35.0)	(139.4)
Server system HW maintenance..........$	0.0	(14.6)	(18.4)	(22.4)	(55.4)
Desktop system HW maintenance........$	0.0	(6.9)	(10.4)	(13.9)	(31.3)
NW & Comm HW maintenance............$	0.0	(4.6)	(6.8)	(9.8)	(21.2)
Total Hardware $	(126.4)	(146.1)	(141.6)	(152.1)	(566.3)
Engineering Design& Mfg Labor					
Initial training - Design engineers..........$	0.0	(19.0)	(14.3)	0.0	(33.3)
Initial training - Manufacturing mgmt......$	(13.0)	(13.0)	0.0	0.0	(26.0)
Design engineering labor....................$	0.0	(6,948.2)	(7,921.0)	(8,504.6)	(23,373.9)
Manufacturing labor..........................$	0.0	(4,673.8)	(5,320.6)	(5,427.0)	(15,421.3)
Change costs / Change mgmt..............$	0.0	(7,221.1)	(7,221.1)	(7,221.1)	(21,663.2)
Total Engr Design & Mfg Labor $	(13.0)	(18,875.1)	(20,476.9)	(21,152.7)	(60,517.6)
IT Support Personnel					
Initial training - IT support...................$	0.0	(20.0)	(20.0)	(20.0)	(60.0)
Install & migration labor, internal..........$	0.0	(58.6)	(59.8)	(61.0)	(179.4)
Continuing training - IT support............$	0.0	(30.0)	(34.0)	(34.0)	(98.0)
SW and HW operations labor..............$	0.0	(234.5)	(239.2)	(234.5)	(708.3)
User help desk................................$	0.0	(46.7)	(47.6)	(48.6)	(142.8)
Total IT Support Personnel $	0.0	(389.8)	(400.6)	(398.1)	(1,188.5)
External Services					
SW install & migration services............$	0.0	0.0	0.0	0.0	0.0
Systems integration services...............$	(5.0)	(12.0)	(12.0)	0.0	(29.0)
Process analysis & mgmt consult.........$	0.0	0.0	0.0	0.0	0.0
Total External Services $	(5.0)	(12.0)	(12.0)	0.0	(29.0)
Total Costs $	(252.6)	(19,582.1)	(21,173.1)	(21,787.7)	(62,795.4)
CASH FLOW SUMMARY (Cash inflows / (outflows))					
Benefits..$	0.0	42,933.5	46,432.6	50,216.9	139,583.0
Costs...$	(252.6)	(19,582.1)	(21,173.1)	(21,787.7)	(62,795.4)
NET CASH FLOW ....$	**(252.6)**	**23,351.5**	**25,259.5**	**28,429.2**	**76,787.6**
Cumulative net cash flow ....$	(252.6)	23,098.9	48,358.4	76,787.6	
Discounted cash flow at 8.0% ....$	(252.6)	21,621.7	21,656.0	22,568.0	65,593.1

Exhibit 4.3 The full value cash flow statement for the Business as Usual Scenario in the Aerofirma Example Case.

Incremental Cash Flow Statement: Proposed Upgrade Scenario

Net Incremental Cash Flow............$	20,555.7
Net Present Value (NPV) at 8.0% ....$	17,330.0
Total Incremental Benefits/Gains......$	26,744.6
Total Incremental Costs.................$	(6,188.9)
Analysis Period...............................	1-Jan-2010 through 31-Dec-2012

$ in 1000s	Yr 0	Yr 1 31 Dec 2010	Yr 2 31 Dec 2011	Yr 3 31 Dec 2012	TOTAL
INCREMENTAL BENEFITS (Cash inflows)					
Gross profits - Product sales ....$	0.0	2,044.5	2,087.4	2,133.1	6,265.0
Avoided cost - Design engr labor........$	0.0	1,839.2	2,709.8	3,189.2	7,738.3
Savings - Change costs / mgmt...........$	0.0	2,940.3	4,410.5	5,390.6	12,741.3
Total Benefits/Gains $	0.0	6,824.0	9,207.7	10,712.9	26,744.6
INCREMENTAL COSTS (Cash outflows)					
Software					
One-time license - Design SW.............$	(79.4)	(23.4)	(44.7)	(60.3)	(207.8)
One-time license - Database SW.........$	(6.9)	0.1	0.1	(3.6)	(10.3)
One-time license - Admin SW.............$	(8.2)	(5.0)	(5.9)	(5.9)	(24.9)
Annual software maintenance.............$	0.0	(10.3)	(14.8)	(23.0)	(48.1)
Total Software $	(94.5)	(38.6)	(65.3)	(92.8)	(291.1)
Hardware					
Server system purchase/upgrade........$	(140.0)	(10.0)	(10.0)	(3.0)	(163.0)
Desktop system purchase/upgrade ....$	(28.0)	(18.0)	1.0	(1.0)	(46.0)
NW & Comm HW purchase/UG..... ....$	0.0	0.0	0.0	0.0	0.0
Server system HW maintenance..........$	0.0	(8.1)	(8.5)	(8.0)	(24.6)
Desktop system HW maintenance........$	0.0	(7.7)	(8.0)	(8.5)	(24.1)
NW & Comm HW maintenance...........$	0.0	(2.3)	(3.6)	(4.1)	(10.1)
Total Hardware $	(168.0)	(46.1)	(29.1)	(24.6)	(267.8)
Engineering Design& Mfg Labor					
Intial training - Design engineers.........$	108.0	(61.0)	(15.8)	(30.0)	1.3
Initial training - Manufacturing mgmt......$	(31.0)	(9.0)	0.0	0.0	(40.0)
Manufacturing labor..........................$	0.0	(1,585.7)	(1,064.1)	(1,276.9)	(3,926.8)
Total Engr Design & Mfg Labor $	77.0	(1,655.7)	(1,079.9)	(1,306.9)	(3,965.5)
IT Support Personnel					
Initial training - Design engineers.........$	(40.0)	20.0	20.0	20.0	20.0
Install & migration labor, internal.........$	0.0	(175.9)	(179.4)	(183.0)	(538.3)
Continuing training - IT support............$	0.0	(36.0)	(32.0)	(32.0)	(100.0)
SW and HW operations labor..............$	0.0	(234.5)	(239.2)	(234.5)	(708.3)
User help desk................................$	0.0	(46.7)	0.0	0.0	(46.7)
Total IT Support Personnel $	(40.0)	(473.1)	(430.6)	(429.5)	(1,373.2)
External Services					
SW install & migration services............$	(48.5)	(35.0)	(35.0)	(20.0)	(120.1)
Systems integration services...............$	(20.7)	(10.0)	(10.0)	(22.0)	(62.7)
Process analysis & mgmt consult.........$	(30.0)	(20.0)	(20.0)	(20.0)	(62.7)
Total External Services $	(99.2)	(65.0)	(65.0)	(62.0)	(245.5)
Total Costs $	(324.7)	(2,278.5)	(1,669.9)	(1,915.8)	(6,188.9)
CASH FLOW SUMMARY (Cash inflows / (outflows))					
Benefits...$	0.0	6,824.0	9,207.7	10,712.9	26,744.6
Costs...$	(324.7)	(2,278.5)	(1,669.9)	(1,915.8)	(6,188.9)
NET CASH FLOW ....$	**(324.7)**	**4,545.5**	**7,537.8**	**8,797.1**	**20,555.7**
Cumulative net cash flow ....$	(324.7)	4,220.8	11,758.6	20,555.7	
Discounted cash flow at 8.0% ....$	(324.7)	4,208.8	6,462.5	6,983.4	17,330.0

Exhibit 4.4 The incremental cash flow statement for the Proposed Upgrade Scenario in the Aerofirma Example Case. Every figure here is the difference between the corresponding full value figures on the Proposed Upgrade Scenario (Exhibit 4.2) and the Business as Usual Scenario (Exhibit 4.3).

Year 0 for Immediate Inflows or Outflows.

The Aerofirma example case looks forward to costs and benefits across a three-year analysis period, 1 January 2010 through 31 December 2012. Year 1 of this period is the calendar year 2010. You may notice, however, the "Year 0" column on the cash flow statements from Exhibits 4.2, 4.3, and 4.4. Notice also that some cost items have cash flow estimates for Year 0. The Year 0 convention is not required but sometimes it can be very helpful for planning spending or incoming funds.

Year 0 represents inflows or ouflows that come immediately at the start of the first analysis year. The major part of Aerofirma's anticipated software purchase is placed in Year 0, for example, as are some initial training costs and other services costs. These cash outflows are technically within Year 1. In deciding which scenario to implement, however, it may be important to see how much funding must be covered when the analysis period starts, and to see that separately from the other Year 1 funds.

Year 0 funds, incidentally, are not discounted for the net present value (NPV) calculations. For Year 0 funds, present value and future value are the same because essentially no time passes before the cash flows.

A good suggestion is to use a Year 0 when management needs to see which inflows and outflows come immediately. Otherwise, omit the Year 0 column and add the immediate events to the rest of Year 1 cash flows.

Where is Projected Income (or Earnings/Profits)?

Projected cash flow figures are the starting point for financial analysis in the business case, rather than "income," for two reasons.

1. For tax-paying companies in private industry, cash flow is a direct measure of financial impact. Income is not.

   When the organization buys an asset with cash, for instance, the entire cash outflow appears on the accounting cash flow statement for that accounting period. Income statements, by contrast, use a number of accounting conventions that mask, or partially obscure the direct financial impact. The same asset purchase impacts the income statement across a number of years as depreciation expense (an accounting convention) that does not reflect the timing of the true cash flow.

2. For non tax paying government organizations, or non profit organizations in education, health care, charities, and other areas, earned income is a non issue. These organizations have budgets, financial limits, and financial goals which can be addressed through the business case cash flow statements, but not through the income statement.

For some cases in private industry, of course, projected income (earnings, or profits) are important. Management will want to see projected income (or contribution to income) for each business case scenario if the purpose of the business case is to address questions like these:

- Will the new product be profitable? How much will it contribute to earnings?
- How will the new product impact profits from our other products?
- Should we change our business model?
- Which new market should we enter?
- Should we enter the after-sales service business?

For these and similar questions, the business case author will first produce cash flow statements for each scenario under consideration, as illustrated here, and then project these into an income statement using the company's business model (or income statement conventions).

Categories for the Cash Flow Statement

Under the main headings "Benefits" and "Costs," the business case author has considerable freedom to choose and arrange other headings and sub headings. In fact, some of this freedom was exercised when the author developed the **Benefits Rationale** (pp. 28-34) and the **Cost Model** (pp. 41-48). The structure of these design blocks should be apparent in the cash flow statements.

Additionally, the author may wish to structure the cash flow statement to create categories that may be important to management. Such categories may show, for instance, differences between

- Capital spending and operating expenses.

  When the case anticipates both kinds of spending, it can be helpful to separate cost items into (1) an "Assets" or "Capital spending" section and (2) an "Operating Expenses" section. The different kinds of spending are planned and managed through different budgets, are reported differently by the accountants, and may be decided by different managers.

- Budgeted funds and non-budgeted funds.

  When the proposal anticipates spending non budgeted funds, these will require a special approval process. In such cases, it is helpful to summarize these costs separately from the budgeted cost items.

- Continuing labor and incremental labor.

  Budgets for continuing labor may be already be approved or at least assumed, whereas requested funding for incremental labor may have to go through an approval process. Here, too, it's helpful if the cash flow statement shows clearly how much of the anticipated labor expenses fall in each category.

- Full time employee labor and part-time or contract labor.

  These labor categories, too, are planned and managed differently, and it may be helpful to see each kind of spending summarized in a section of its own. The two kinds of labor bring different kinds of costs and responsibilities for management. Moreover, management usually has more flexibility to add or subtract from the contract or part time labor force on short notice.

Should Business Case Projections Include Tax Consequences?

In a tax-paying organization, most cash inflows and outflows ultimately contribute to a tax impact of some kind.[1] For instance:

- Cash inflows that contribute to operating gains increase the tax liability on operating income.
- Cash outflows that reduce operating gains or create an operating loss contribute to a tax savings.
- Cash inflows that represent capital gains may create a tax liability.
- Asset depreciation expenses (reported on the income statement) create a tax savings.

These tax consequences do represent real cash flow for the organization. Tax consequences are typically not included in the business case cash flow statements, however. The reason for the omission, probably, is that adding tax consequences to cash flow estimates "muddies the waters," that is, makes it harder to see and compare the direct cash flow consequences under different scenarios. Adding tax consequences to the picture reduces the apparent magnitude of both gains and losses.

There are a two kinds of situations in a tax paying organization, however, where the author will certainly want to "factor in" cash flow tax consequences.

- If the different action scenarios under consideration predict different impacts on reported income—differences that are large and important to management—then tax consequences are important addition to the cash flow summaries.

- If different action alternatives are under consideration *because* they have different tax consequences, those consequences obviously need to appear in the cash flow statements. When a major capital acquisition is under consideration, for instance, the "Lease" vs. "Buy" question is often decided on the basis of different tax consequences under leasing versus buying.

Where do the Cash Flow Figures Come From?

This brief book focuses on "what" belongs in a business case, and "why." Explaining how cost and benefit projections are developed is beyond the scope intended here. Still, it is worth mentioning a few important points about cost/benefit estimation and illustrating, in the next section, how a cost figure can be modeled and estimated for one line item example. Some important considerations to remember include these points:

---

1. For more examples and in-depth coverage on cash flow statement structure and tax consequences in the business case, see *The Business Case Guide* or the spreadsheet tool, Financial Modeling Pro™. Information on these items is available at www.solutionmatrix.com.

- Outcomes of an action called "benefits" are given financial value because they contribute to meeting business objectives.

  Meeting objectives has value. In the **Benefits Rational** block (pp. 28-34), the benefits strategy outlined there begins by identifying business objectives addressed by the action, explaining how progress towards the objective is measured (made tangible), and setting a financial value on reaching the objective.

- When proposed actions target increased sales revenues, the analysis must recognize that increased revenues usually bring increased costs as well.

  Projected sales revenues should go into the cash flow statement as benefits only when all the costs of generating those revenues are included in the cost model. Otherwise, it is better to enter projected "Gross profits" as benefits, because these figures *do* reflect the direct costs of producing sales revenues (as in the Aerofirma example).

- Many kinds of benefits normally take time to "ramp up" or reach target value.

  Increased sales from a marketing campaign, or increased productivity from employee training, for instance, will take time to reach their target values. When estimating annual cash flows, the author should build in a learning curve, or "ramp" showing how such benefits will maximize over time.

- The simplest and most certain kinds of cost estimates are usually those that come from vendor proposals. Vendor-provided cost figures can often be entered directly into line item cost estimates.

- The majority of cost item cash flow estimates result from multiplying an assumed number of resource units required, times the assumed cost per unit

- Labor costs for the business case are estimated as "units required" times "cost per unit," where the unit is a measure of person time such as FTE (full time equivalent) person hours, days, or years.

  For the business case the cost per FTE is taken as the salary plus overhead costs paid by the employer. The total is the real cost borne by the employer.

  If the organization's overhead rate is 25% and an employee's annual salary is $60,000 for Year 1, the projected Year 1 cash outflow for that employee is $75,000. (Cash Flow Cost = Salary * (1 + Overhead rate)).

Example: Modeling and Estimating Initial Training Costs

Most cost and benefit items are estimated from *assumptions*. The author is predicting the future, after all, and strictly speaking, everything we know about the future is really an assumption. This means that predicted cash flows are based on information that comes with uncertainty (measuring and minimizing uncertainty are central objectives in the **Risk and Sensitivity Analysis Section** of the Report).

To show how assumptions can be used to reach cost estimate values, consider for instance a cost item from the Aerofirma case, "Initial Training - Design Engineers." The business case author must produce cash flow estimates for this cost item for each scenario, for each year of the analysis period.

- In the cash flow statement for Business as Usual, this item has a 0 value in all years. In that scenario, there is no new design system to train for.
- Non zero cash flow estimates are needed for the same item in the Proposed Upgrade and Combination Proposal scenarios. Here, engineers will need training before they can begin using the upgraded system.

Before attempting to estimate cost figure, the author will very likely consult the company's training manager and software vendor to answer as many questions as possible about how the training will take place and what it attempts to achieve: Will this be classroom training or on-line self-study? If this is classroom training, will it be done onsite or will participants be sent to an off site training facility? Does the course already exist or must it be developed? What are the training objectives for participants? What are their current skill levels and what skills do they need to acquire? And so on. In the Aerofirma case it was agreed that:

- Training will be delivered in classroom sessions.
- Participants will train at an off site training facility.
- The required course exists, and is purchased by hiring a professional training instructor to deliver the course. There will also be a daily training fee per participant.
- Somewhere between 6 and 14 days of classroom instruction will be required for each participant.

Given these starting assumptions, how does the author go on to estimate actual cost figures? In this example, you should begin to appreciate that cost estimates like this can be approached in many different ways, and the choice of estimating method really depends on:

- The importance of this item, relative to other cost and benefit items (that is, whether a relatively large or relatively small amount of money is involved.)
- How much uncertainty in projected results the author and audience are willing to accept.
- The time and resources available to the author for research and analysis on this item.

There may be a very simple and easy answer to the training cost questions: The vendor, for instance, may have information on actual training costs at other companies, with similar installations and similar participants, and those figures may be acceptable as training cost estimates. Or, industry standard training cost averages may be available from other sources. No such information was available to Aerofirma, however. Because the training costs were expected to be large, and because the training budget was already under pressure—with little margin for error in the projected costs—the author chose to perform a more detailed estimate based on important assumptions. This began with an assumption that initial training costs would consist of three components:

- **Participant costs:** The fees for each participant's training days.
- **Instructor costs:** The cost of hiring the professional training instructor for course delivery.
- **Facilities costs:** The cost of renting the classroom and laboratories with engineering workstations.

In order to develop the model from here, the author used a visual technique called influence diagramming, illustrated in Exhibit 4.5 (next page).[2] Diagramming begins on the *right* side with a hexagon representing the target value—the initial training cost to be estimated. A text box at the upper left, labeled "Scenarios" is a reminder that this cost figure must be estimated for each scenario in the case. The three main components mentioned above are really "assumptions," or "uncertainties". These are placed in ovals, immediately to the left of the value hexagon. The arrows from each oval to the hexagon mean that the value is influenced by these uncertainties.

Now the author asks: "What would I need to know or assume, in order to estimate participant costs? To estimate instructor costs? Facilities costs? With a little thought (and help from the training manager), the author identified ten more assumptions that contribute to these estimates:

1. Number of participants trained
2. Instructor salary per day
3. The duration of each training class (in days)
4. The maximum size of each class
5. Participant training fee per day
6. Facilities costs per day
7. The instructor cost per class
8. Cost per participant
9. The number of training classes given
10. Training facilities costs per class

These assumptions (uncertainties) are placed in ovals to the left of the value hexagon and to the left of the first three ovals (see Exhibit 4.5). Now the author attempts to determine

- Which uncertainties are "Input" assumptions? Values for these assumptions will be entered into the model directly.
- Which uncertainties are derived from other assumptions?

The visual diagram makes it easy to sort out the relationships among assumptions and then build these relationships into spreadsheet formulas. The author simply draws an arrow from one oval to another wherever one assumption influences another. This shows, for instance that "Number of training classes given" (9 above) is derived from two input assumptions, "Number of participants trained" (1) and "Maximum size of each class" (4). With this approach, assump-

---

2. For a complete introduction to influence diagramming for cost and benefit estimates, see *The Definitive Guide to Getting Your Budget Approved.* Spreadsheet model building is covered in depth with the Microsoft Excel-based tool, Financial Modeling Pro™. For more on these resources see www.solutionmatrix.com.

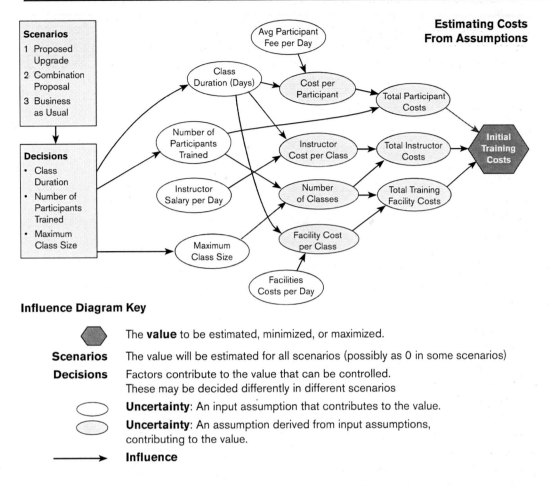

Estimating Costs From Assumptions

Influence Diagram Key

The **value** to be estimated, minimized, or maximized.

Scenarios The value will be estimated for all scenarios (possibly as 0 in some scenarios)

Decisions Factors contribute to the value that can be controlled.
These may be decided differently in different scenarios

Uncertainty: An input assumption that contributes to the value.

Uncertainty: An assumption derived from input assumptions, contributing to the value.

Influence

Exhibit 4.5 Using an influence diagram to model assumptions and influences that produce a cost value. See text for explanation.

tions 1-6 above turn out to be input assumptions (in white ovals) and assumptions 7-10 are derived (in shaded ovals).

To complete the influence diagram, the author also identifies the assumptions that can be controlled directly, or which may represent arbitrary choices. These are listed as "Decisions" in a box under the Scenarios box. Influence arrows from the decision box to the named assumptions remind management which assumptions they may wish to manipulate, later, in an attempt to minimize costs.

With the influence diagram completed, the ovals and arrows are turned into formulas that can be implemented in a spreadsheet model, as suggested in Exhibit 4.6 (next page).

Actually making the Initial Training Cost Estimate, then becomes a matter of choosing values for the input assumptions. Exhibit 4.6 also shows how the inputs summary, intermediate results (derived assumptions), and final output might look in spreadsheet form. Here, the figures represent "Year 0" estimated training costs for the Proposed Upgrade scenario.

Assumptions (Uncertainties)	Assumption Names	Expected Value	Microsoft Excel Formula
1 Number of partcipants trained..........NumParticipTrained		40	
2 Instructor salary per day ($)...................InstSalaryDay		$1,200	
3 Class duration (Days).............................ClassDuration		10	Input assumptions, entered directly as numbers
4 Maximum class size...........................MaxClassSize		10	
5 Participant training fee per day($)...........ParticipFeeDay		$100	
6 Facilites cost per day ($)...................FacilitiesCostDay		$500	
7 Instructor cost per class ($).....................InstCostClass		$12,000	= InstSalaryDay * ClassDuration
8 Cost per participant ($)...........................ParticipCost		$1,000	= ClassDuration * ParticipFeeDay
9 Number of classes................................NumClasses		4	= ROUNDUP (NumParticipTrained / MaxClassSize, 0)
10 Training facilities cost per class ($).........FacilCostClass		$5,000	= ClassDuration * FacilitiesCostDay
Total participant costs ($)................ TotalParticipCosts		$40,000	= ParticipCost * NumParticipTrained
Total instructor costs $)........................... TotalInstCost		$48,000	= InstCostClass * NumClasses
Total Training Facility Costs ($)...... TotalTrainFacilCosts		$20,000	= FacilCostClass * ClassDuration * NumClasses
Initial Training Costs		**$108,000**	= TotalParticipCosts + TotalInstCost + TotalTrainFacilCosts

Exhibit 4.6 Turning the influence diagram model into spreadsheet formulas. Input assumptions are entered directly as numbers (lines 1-6). Derived assumptions are built from the inputs (lines 7-10 and three main component costs below them) using the Microsoft Excel formulas shown at right. In the spreadsheet implementation, assumption cells have been assigned the names shown at the left of each cell, allowing the author to write formulas using these names. Notice the Excel ROUNDUP function for derived assumption 9, Number of Classes. This ensures that the number of classes will be an integer number.

Analysis of Results

The **Analysis of results** develops information from the cash flow statements just presented. A broader analysis in the next major section of the report (**Risk and Sensitivity Analysis**) goes further, to examine sensitivity of results to changing assumptions and to measure risks. Here, however, the focus is on the important financial metrics identified in the **Methods Section.**

The analysis normally presents a summary of financial metrics based on the net cash flow stream for each scenario. These metrics appear in Exhibit 4.7 (next page) showing how the Aerofirma analysis summary might appear. The tables and graphs allow the reader to compare basic financial metrics from three full value and both incremental cash flow statements (three of the five cash flow statements appeared earlier as Exhibits 4.2, 4.3, and 4.4). Notice especially:

- Full value statements and summary metrics are useful for planning purposes, e.g., for fore-casting revenues, margins, expenses, or capital spending under each scenario.

  In Exhibit 4.7, the full value scenarios are compared on the basis of net cash flow, net present value (NPV), total benefits, and total costs.

- Incremental cash flow statements and metrics are especially helpful when deciding which scenario to implement. The incremental scenarios show just what changes (relative to Business as Usual) when either proposal scenario is implemented.

  Here, the two proposal scenarios can be compared to each other, with respect to net incremental cash flow, NPV of net incremental cash flow, incremental benefits, incremental costs, and 3-year return on investment (ROI).

Summary of Financial Results

Analysis Period: 1 January 2010 - 31 December 2012

$ in 1,000s	Full Value Cash Flow Scenarios		
	Proposed Upgrade	Combination Proposal	Business as Usual
Net Cash Flow	$97,343.3	$95,973.8	$76,787.6
Net Present Value (NPV) at 8%	$82,923.1	$81,332.0	$65,781.0
Total Benefits/Gains	$145,848.0	$165,667.8	$139,583.0
Total Costs	($48,504.7)	($69,694.0)	($62,795.4)

$ in 1,000s	Incremental Cash Flow	
	Proposed Upgrade	Combination Proposal
Incremental Net Cash Flow	$20,555.7	$19,186.2
NPV, Incremental Cash Flow	$17,330.0	$15,738.9
Incremental Benefits/Gains	$26,744.6	$26,084.8
Incremental Costs	($6,188.9)	($6,898.6)
3 Yr Return on Investment (ROI)	432.1%	378.1%

Annual Cash Flow

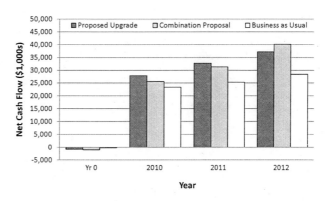

Annual Incremental Cash Flow

Exhibit 4.7 Summary of financial results from the 5 cash flow statements in the Aerofirma case.

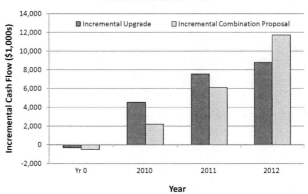

When reporting cash flow results and their direct analysis in the **Business Results Section**, it is good form to minimize narrative interpretation. The idea, after all, is to give the numbers a chance to speak for themselves first, before the author's interpretations and recommendations are added. Interpretation and elaboration are more appropriate in the following sections, **Sensitivity and Risk Analysis**, and **Conclusions and Recommendations.**

Providing readers with a comprehensive cost summary and analysis as shown in Exhibit 4.8 (next page) can also be helpful. Here the total 3-year costs for each cost model cell are brought together, organized in the same framework as the cost model (repeated in the upper part of the Exhibit). This format can be used for full value cash flow (page middle) and incremental cash flow (page bottom).

Summarizing costs in this way puts the spotlight on aspects of the cost outlook that might not be apparent or easily seen in the cash flow statements. The cost model summary can be especially helpful when row and column totals are added in the margins. The full value cost summary for the Proposed upgrade scenario, for instance, shows that almost 91% of the 3-year costs are Engineering and Manufacturing "People Costs."

Non Financial Results

Non financial benefits and costs often seem to present a special challenge to business case authors. When faced with the need to make tangible, estimate, and value outcomes like "Improved safety," or "Damaged brand image," for instance, many simply throw up their hands and omit such outcomes from the case. Others include them, but turn them into second class citizens in the **Business Results Section**, by giving them cursory treatment under headings like "Soft Benefits" or "Intangibles." Both approaches can be misleading and inappropriate especially when the non financial outcomes are important.

The cash flow statements and financial analyses are blind to non financial business outcomes, and for that reason, authors are encouraged to make a serious effort to develop a credible, acceptable financial value for all important benefit and cost outcomes, even when the outcomes are defined and measured first in non financial terms. The **Benefits Rationale** block (pp. 28-34) presents a reasoning and practical steps that often make this possible.

Nevertheless, not all important costs and benefits yield to this treatment. Some of them simply cannot be given a financial value that has meaning. This seems to happen especially often when the outcomes are benefits for an initiative or project in a government or non profit organization. In such cases, the author can still apply the benefits rationale steps up to a point—the point where value is stated with a financial figure. The task then is to establish value, or importance, in non financial terms.

When reporting non financial costs and benefits in the **Business Results Section**, it may be helpful to restate here some definitions and some of the main points from the benefits rationale. Remember, first, that costs and benefits for the business case are best defined in terms of business objectives.

> **Benefit:** A result that contributes *towards* meeting a business objective
> **Cost:** A result that works *against* meeting a business objective.

COST MODEL FOR ALL SCENARIOS

		ACQUISITION & CHANGE System Acquisition, Migration, Upgrade & Deployment Costs	OPERATIONS Continuing Operating Costs
RESOURCES	Software	• One-time license - Design SW • One-time license - Database SW • One-time license - Admin SW	• SW Maintenance costs
	Hardware	• Server systems purchase/UG • Desktop systems purchase/UG • NW/Comm HW purchase/UG	• Server systems maintenance • Desktop systems maintenance • NW/Comm maintenance
	Eng / Mfr Labor	• Initial training - Design engineers • Initial training - Mfr mgmt	• Design engineering labor • Manufacturing labor • Change costs / Change mgmt
	IT Support Personnel	• Initial training - IT support • SW install & migr labor (internal)	• Continuing training - IT support • SW and HW operations labor • User Help Desk
	External Services	• SW install & migration servces • Process analysis & mgmt consult	• Systems integration services

THREE YEAR COST SUMMARY - PROPOSED UPGRADE SCENARIO

$ in 1000s	ACQUISITION & CHANGE System Acquisition, Migration, Upgrade & Deployment Costs	OPERATIONS Continuing Operating Costs	Total	% of Grand Total
Software	(634)	(151)	(785)	1.6%
Hardware	(667)	(167)	(834)	1.7%
E/M Labor	(98)	(43,906)	(44,004)	90.7%
IT Support	(758)	(1,804)	(2,562)	5.3%
Ext Svcs	(229)	(92)	(320)	0.7%
Total	(2,385)	(46,119)	(48,505)	
% Grand Total	4.9%	95.1%		100.0%

THREE YEAR INCREMENTAL COSTS - PROPOSED UPGRAGE SCENARIO
Incremental Costs = Proposed Upgrade Scenario Costs - Business as Usual Costs

$ in 1000s	ACQUISITION & CHANGE System Acquisition, Migration, Upgrade & Deployment Costs	OPERATIONS Continuing Operating Costs	Total
Software	(243)	(48)	(291)
Hardware	(209)	(59)	(268)
E/M Labor	(39)	16,553	16,514
IT Support	(518)	(855)	(1,373)
Ext Svcs	(229)	(63)	(291)
Total	(1,238)	15,528	14,291

Exhibit 4.8 Cost analysis summary for the Aerofirma Proposed Upgrade scenario, showing full cost totals (middle) and total incremental costs (bottom).

If the outcome is to be called a benefit, the author should also report the following:

1. The outcome (benefit) and how it is measured in tangible terms.
2. The objective addressed and how that is measured in tangible terms.
3. The target for the objective (in those tangible terms)
4. How and why the benefit contributes to meeting the objective.
5. How much progress towards the target can be expected from the benefit.
6. Evidence that meeting the objective's target is important and/or has value.

Exhibit 4.9 (next page) shows what these steps might look like, for an example benefit (shorter customer telephone wait time) that contributes to meeting a business objective (improved customer satisfaction). Especially critical steps are No. 4, showing in credible terms how and why the benefit contributes to meeting the objective, and No. 6, Showing that meeting the objective's target is important.

Regarding step 6, establishing value or importance for the objective (and therefore, the benefit), Exhibit 4.10 (page 70) illustrates an approach that can be very effective when scenario business results include both financial and non financial benefits: comparing all benefits in a scenario with each other, on a common basis. These may represent major corporate objectives, which should ultimately translate into lower costs and increased revenues. The graph summarizes the consensus view of a large international bank's Executive Committee after considering an IT action—upgrading local area networks and personal productivity software in branch offices for the use of loan officers. The Committee used a "score and weight" consensus-building technique to rate the relative contributions of various benefits to the bank's overall strategic business goals.[3]

Surprisingly, in this exercise, the top rating went to a non-financial benefit: "Improved company image," while one benefit that was quantified in financial terms (Increased productivity) finished fifth out of the five benefits considered. Of course, everyone expects the non financial benefits listed here to help deliver revenues and profits, but the value of the IT contribution to these goals was impossible for this group to measure comfortably in financial terms. Ratings such as those in Exhibit 4.10 reminded everyone that even non-financial benefits are important and worth paying for.

---

3. Methods for building a consensus view with a score and weight approach, are described in *The Business Case Guide*. Information on the *Guide* is available at www.solutionmatrix.com.

Customer Satisfaction:	
An initiative designed to reduce average telephone wait time on customer service calls	

Proposed actions.	• Upgrade phone switching hardware and software in call center. • Increase number of call center agents on duty by 20%. • Improve agent productivity through training, and through improved information access software.
1. The outcome (Benefit).	Shorter customer wait time on customer service hotline. *Wait time is measured as: average wait time, in seconds, between automatic call answering and first contact with call center agent.* *Expected change:* *Business as Usual Scenario: No change from current avg 180 seconds.* *Proposal Scenario: Average wait time drops from 180 to 15 seconds.*
2. Business objective(s)s addressed.	Improved customer satisfaction. *Customer satisfaction is measured in terms of:* • Satisfaction ratings on customer satisfaction surveys. • Number of customer complaints/compliments per month. • Repeat business rate (% customers who buy again). • Referral business rate (% customers referred by other customers).
3. Targets for the objective.	• Target: % of customers giving top rating goes from 40% to 60%. • Target: Number of monthly customer complaints decreases 50%. • Target: Repeat business rate goes from 50% to 75%. • Target: Referral business rate goes from 10% to 20%.
4. How or why benefit contributes to objective.	• Over 40% of current customer complaints mention excessive wait time or other call handling problems as source of dissatisfaction. • Currently, 10% of incoming calls are abandoned by customer, before speaking to live agent.
5. How much progress towards target can be expected from the benefit, in each scenario?	Estimated impacts, Business as Usual Scenario: None. Estimated impacts, Proposal scenario: • Customers giving highest ratings: 50% of targeted improvement. • Number of customer complaints: 40% of targeted decrease. • Repeat business rate: 20% of targeted increase. • Referral business rate: 50% of targeted increase.
6. Evidence that meeting the objective is important or has value.	• Industry surveys cite "Customer Satisfaction with after sales service" as the Number 1 reason for repeat business and for referring others • Our company currently ranks third among our competitors in customer satisfaction, as measured by survey scores.

Exhibit 4.9 Establishing the legitimacy of a non financial benefit (shorter customer wait time) in terms of a non financial business objective (Improved customer satisfaction). Both the benefit and the business objective it address must be measurable in tangible terms. Especially critical steps are No. 4, demonstrating how or why the benefit contributes to the objective, and No. 6, showing that reaching the objective is important.

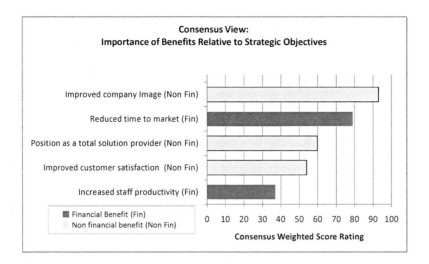

Exhibit 4.10. The consensus view of one bank's Executive Committee: A score and weight rating method was used to compare financial benefits (indicated with Fin) and non financial benefits (Non Fin). Consensus weights are the relative contributions of benefits to the bank's overall strategic business objectives.

Chapter 4 Summary

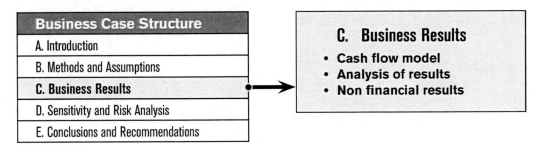

Business Case Structure
A. Introduction
B. Methods and Assumptions
C. Business Results
D. Sensitivity and Risk Analysis
E. Conclusions and Recommendations

C. Business Results

- **Cash flow model**
- **Analysis of results**
- **Non financial results**

- Financial results under each scenario appear in a cash flow model. This includes a set of cash flow statements—one full value statement for each scenario, as well as incremental cash flow statements.

- Cash flow statements summarize predicted cash inflows and outflows for cost items (from the Cost Model block) and benefit items (from the Benefits Rationale).

- Cost savings and avoided costs can be seen by comparing two full value cash flow statements. The incremental cash flow statement performs this comparison by subtracting business as usual values from proposal scenario values. Cost savings and avoided costs appear on the incremental cash flow statements as cash inflows (benefits).

- Cost and benefit cash flow figures are derived from assumptions. Influence diagramming is one effective tool for modeling the relationships among assumptions and their contributions to cost and benefit items.

- Financial metrics are developed from analysis of cash flow statement figures. Some of the most basic and informative financial metrics include net cash flow, total cost, net present value (NPV), and return on investment (ROI).

- Important non financial business results should be included in the case where they can be described in tangible terms, and where the author can establish their importance.

Chapter 5

Sensitivity and Risk Analysis

Almost all business cases involve uncertainty because they project results into the future. The "Business Results" blocks in the previous section represent the author's estimated most likely outcomes, but no matter how solid the methods and analysis behind the results, audiences will have other questions, such as:

- *What happens if some of the assumptions change?*
- *Just how likely is this set of results? How likely are other results?*
- *What must happen in order to obtain the results presented here?*
- *What can we do to maximize returns and minimize costs?*

Questions like these are addressed with sensitivity and risk analysis.

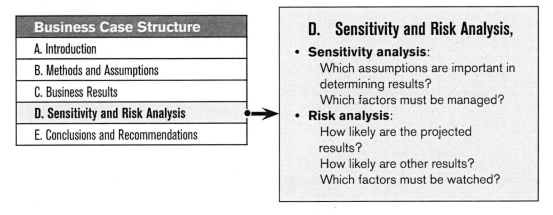

Business Case Structure
A. Introduction
B. Methods and Assumptions
C. Business Results
D. Sensitivity and Risk Analysis
E. Conclusions and Recommendations

D.   Sensitivity and Risk Analysis,
- **Sensitivity analysis**:
   Which assumptions are important in determining results?
   Which factors must be managed?
- **Risk analysis**:
   How likely are the projected results?
   How likely are other results?
   Which factors must be watched?

Business results in the previous section provide decision makers and planners *some* of the information they need to choose an action scenario or predict incoming and outgoing funds. In the Aerofirma example, expected 3-year net cash flow and ROI were higher for the Proposed Upgrade scenario than for the Combination Proposal. However, no one should view that information alone as sufficient for recommending a course of action.

Those responsible for deciding which scenario to implement also need to know the likelihood that results will be close to the predicted values and the likelihood they could be quite different. They also need to know which contingencies or critical success factors must be managed to which target levels, in order to bring in predicted results. And they need to know which risk factors need to be watched carefully—risks that would upset predictions. Sensitivity and risk analysis provide such information.

Sensitivity Analysis

Remember that the cash flow model and cash flow metrics are the product of many assumptions. For a case with a set of cost and benefit items similar to the Aerofirma example, overall financial results may depend on *hundreds* of assumptions about such things as

- Predicted business volume or customer demand.
- Sales revenue forecasts.
- Availability of funding.
- Market growth rate.
- Population growth rate.
- Competitor business volume in the same market.
- Salary levels.
- International currency exchange rates.
- The rate of inflation.
- Prices of raw materials or commodities.
- Prices of assets (e.g., land, buildings, stock, mineral rights).
- Time required for staff to learn new skills.
- Time required to develop and ship new products.
- Changes in government regulation.

Sensitivity analysis asks "What happens if these assumptions change?" and "Which assumptions are most important in controlling results?" Knowing which of these assumptions are important in controlling financial results enables the author to make very specific practical recommendations on how to manage the proposed actions so as to maximize results.

The objective in **risk analysis** is to measure the probabilities that different results occur. For each scenario, the author predicts outcomes for such things as net cash flow, NPV, ROI, or total cost. An infinite number of other outcomes are possible, however, because predicted results depend on assumptions and assumptions like those above come with uncertainty. One scenario might come with a higher predicted net cash flow than another, for instance, but that same scenario might also have a lower probability of delivering predicted results. Risk analysis enables decision makers to weigh expected returns against risks for each alternative.

Making Assumptions: Point Estimates vs. Ranges

Sensitivity and risk questions can be asked about individual cost and benefit items as well as financial metrics for the whole scenario. The approach in both cases is the same, but the principles involved are easier to illustrate first with a single-item example. Consider the example from the previous chapter showing how Aerofirma's initial training cost estimate was derived from 6 input assumptions (Exhibits 4.5 and 4.6, pp. 60-64). A slightly-expanded version of Exhibit 4.6 is repeated on the next page as Exhibit 5.1.

What is new here are the "Min" and "Max" columns for each input assumption, on either side of the "Expected Value" column. Now, the author provides a *range* of possible values for each assumption along with the most likely point value. The author originally estimated the number of trainees as 40, and this is still viewed as the most likely value for this assumption. Discussions with engineering management, however, determined that the actual number could be as low as 30 (perhaps because some engineers might already have the necessary skills). On the other hand, the number could be as high as 50, if there is turnover in the engineering department during the coming year. In any case, if the author is confident that the actual number will be no less than 30 or more than 50, then the uncertainty associated with this input assump-

Assumptions (Uncertainties)	Assumption Names	Min	Expected Value	Max	Microsoft Excel Formulas
1 Number of partcipants trained.....NumParticipTrained		30	40	50	
2 Instructor salary per day ($)............. InstSalaryDay		$1,000	$1,200	$1,500	
3 Class duration (Days)..................... ClassDuration		6	10	14	Input assumptions,
4 Maximum class size....................... MaxClassSize		7	10	14	entered directly as numbers
5 Participant training fee per day ($).... ParticipFeeDay		$60	$100	$150	
6 Facilites cost per pay ($)............. FacilitiesCostDay		$450	$500	$600	
7 Instructor cost per class ($)............................InstCostClass			$12,000		= InstSalaryDay * ClassDuration
8 Cost per participant ($)....................................ParticipCost			$1,000		= ClassDuration * ParticipFeeDay
9 Number of classes..NumClasses			4		= ROUNDUP(NumParticipTrained/MaxClassSize, 0)
10 Training facilities cost per class ($) ....FacilCostClass			$5,000		= ClassDuration * FacilitiesCostDay
Total participant costs ($)..........................TotalParticipCosts			$40,000		= ParticipCost * NumParticipTrained
Total instructor costs $)....................................TotalInstCost			$48,000		= InstCostClass * NumClasses
Total Training Facility Costs ($)..............TotalTrainFacilCosts			$20,000		= FacilCostClass * NumClasses
Initial Training Costs			$108,000		= TotalParticipCosts+TotalInstCost+TotalTrainFacilCosts

Exhibit 5.1 Modeling initial training costs from assumptions. This extract from a spreadsheet model is Identical to Exhibit 4.6, except for the added "Min" and "Max" columns on either side of "Expected value" for each input assumption. Risk and sensitivity analysis begin by assigning a range of values to each input assumption.

tion has just become measurable. Uncertainty for the model's output (initial training costs) becomes measurable, as well, when all input assumptions have ranges like this.

When working in an environment where there are differences of opinion, incidentally, it can be much easier to get different people to agree on a range of possible assumption values, than on a single point estimate. When some opinions expect a higher value and others expect a lower value, it may be possible to get agreement on a range that covers all opinions, acknowledging that whatever single value is chosen as the "Expected Value," it is likely to be off target, either by a little or by a lot.

Simple Sensitivity Analysis

When assumptions and output value are implemented in a spreadsheet model, such as Exhibit 5.1 above, there is a very simple way to ask the basic sensitivity question "What happens if assumptions change?" So-called simple sensitivity analysis is nothing more than taking the input assumptions, one by one, and substituting minimum, expected, and maximum values into the model and recording the resulting output value each time. When this has been done for one input assumption, the expected value for that assumptions is reinserted in the model, and testing proceeds with the next assumption. The results of such an exercise are summarized in Exhibit 5.2 (next page) as both a table and a graph.

"Sensitivity" refers to the behavior of the predicted value, in this case initial training costs. Both table and graph show that the predicted value is more sensitive to changes in some assumptions then to changes in others. As the input assumption "Class duration" is taken from it's minimum to maximum values, the predicted output training cost figure changes by $86,000. The difference between cost results at minimum and maximum values for the assumption is shown in the "Delta" column of the table. By contrast, when the input assumption "Facilities cost per day" moves from its minimum to its maximum, the output training cost

Simple Sensitivity Analysis

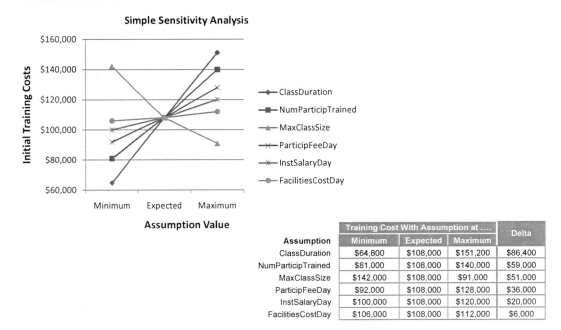

Assumption	Training Cost With Assumption at			Delta
	Minimum	Expected	Maximum	
ClassDuration	$64,800	$108,000	$151,200	$86,400
NumParticipTrained	$81,000	$108,000	$140,000	$59,000
MaxClassSize	$142,000	$108,000	$91,000	$51,000
ParticipFeeDay	$92,000	$108,000	$128,000	$36,000
InstSalaryDay	$100,000	$108,000	$120,000	$20,000
FacilitiesCostDay	$106,000	$108,000	$112,000	$6,000

Exhibit 5.2 Simple sensitivity analysis: The sensitivity of predicted initial training costs to changes in assumptions. These results are based on the spreadsheet model in Exhibit 5.1. The table records the predicted training cost as each assumption is taken from minimum value, to expected value, to maximum value. "Deltas" in the table's right column show the training cost change across the range for each assumption. In the graph, a large Delta shows up as a curve with a steeper slope and a small Delta leads to a curve with a flatter slope.

figure changes by only $6,000. Apparently, class duration is more powerful in controlling this result than facilities cost per day. Sensitivity measured this way can also be seen in the graph above the table. When two assumptions are compared, the one whose curve has the steeper slope is the more powerful.

Simple sensitivity analysis is easy to perform and it is suggested as a first step towards providing a basis for recommendations and conclusion, yet, as an analysis tool, it is flawed and potentially misleading. Nevertheless it is recommended for the following reasons:

- Simple sensitivity analysis as illustrated here, allows the author to test the "rationality" of financial models. If the test produces results behavior that is unexpected or unexplainable, that may indicate that the financial model (formulas and assumptions) needs re-work.
- Simple sensitivity analysis allows the author to address a few "What if?" questions in the **Recommendations and Conclusions Section.** "What if," for instance, "Productivity improvements are only 50% of the assumed value?" "What if the price of oil goes to twice what was assumed?"

Nevertheless, on statistical grounds, simple sensitivity analysis is not a fully acceptable predictor of future results or a fully reliable measure of sensitivity to assumptions. Some of the reasons for this judgement are:

- Simple sensitivity analysis holds all assumptions constant except the one being tested at the time. In reality, it is likely that all assumptions will change from the assumed values in the future.
- Simple sensitivity analysis, as shown, gives equal weight (equal importance) to all assumption values between "Min" and "Max." In reality, for most assumptions, values are more likely close to the "Expected value" than to end points of each range.
- In reality, some of the input assumptions are probably correlated with each other, that is, they tend to change together in predictable ways. For instance, in some training facilities, the daily cost for facilities is correlated with the class size (especially if meals and refreshments are included). Simple sensitivity analysis does not recognize the impacts of such correlations.

Despite these problems, the method is very frequently used in business case analysis today. The reason, probably, are that simple sensitivity analysis is easy to perform and easy to understand. Probably also, not everyone finds the limitations above obvious or compelling.

Sensitivity Analysis with Monte Carlo Simulation

A better approach to sensitivity analysis is to analyze business case financial models with a technique called Monte Carlo simulation,[1] a method that does not have the limitations mentioned above. This approach, moreover, provides a very useful risk analysis along with the sensitivity information.

Monte Carlo simulation also uses a working spreadsheet model, like the example in Exhibit 5.1, where an output result (e.g., initial training costs) results from a number of input assumptions. In this approach, however, the output forecast is recorded after *all* input assumptions are allowed to change at once. The process of changing all assumptions and recording the output value is repeated thousands of times, until a picture emerges showing the full range of possible outputs, the probabilities of different outputs, and contributions of individual assumptions to the output results.

As you might expect, Monte Carlo simulation requires simulation software designed for the purpose. Fortunately, there are a wide range of simulation products available, across a wide range of prices, and Monte Carlo capability is also found in many of the popular comprehensive statistical or financial software systems. Fortunately, also, most of these products are very "user friendly," recognizing that most people do not remember very much from the

---

1. The method is called Monte Carlo simulation because it uses assumptions about probabilities—the same probability theory that applies on the gaming tables in Monte Carlo. More background on Monte Carlo simulation and its use in business case analysis is presented in *The Business Case Guide* and *The Definitive Guide to Getting Your Budget Approved*. Information on these books is available at www.solutionmatrix.com.

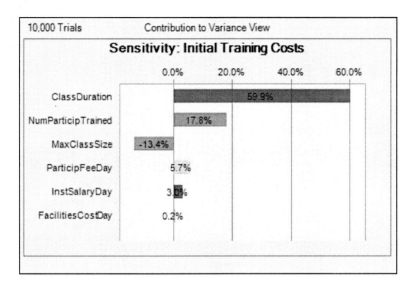

Exhibit 5.2 Sensitivity analysis for one cost item, from Monte Carlo simulation. Here, the relative magnitude of each assumption's contribution to the output value can be compared to the contributions of other assumptions. The direction of the bars (left or right) also shows the sign of the relationship between assumption and results. A positive direction (pointing right), such as shown for class duration, means that as class duration increases, Initial training costs also increase. (Examples in this book are produced by Crystal Ball®, a product of Oracle Corporation). .

basic statistics course they may have taken once long ago. Examples in this book illustrate the use of one such product, Crystal Ball®, a Microsoft Excel Add-in from Oracle Corporation.

Monte Carlo simulation provides a statistically valid risk and sensitivity analysis, such as the sensitivity results shown in Exhibit 5.2 (above). You may notice that the same six assumptions line up in order of importance exactly as they did in the simple sensitivity analysis. Here, however, the length and direction of the bars provides more information about the contribution of each assumption to the initial training cost figure. The input assumption, class duration, for instance, has more than three times the statistical contribution to initial training costs than the next most important assumption, number of participants trained. The positive direction of the bar (pointing to the right) for class duration shows that as class duration increases, initial training costs also increase. The negative contribution (left pointing bar) of the maximum class size assumption shows that as class size increases, initial training costs *decrease*.

One very important finding in this example, is that the three most important contributors to initial training cost are factors that can be controlled to some extent by management. (These factors are listed as "Decisions" in the influence diagram, Exhibit 4.5, pp. 63.) This finding will appear again, later in this chapter, under "Maximizing Results and Minimizing Uncertainty." It will also be turned into practical suggestions for management in the **Conclusions and Recommendations Section**.

The same principles apply when the sensitivity analysis takes on the full cash flow model for the case, including full value and incremental statements. Exhibit 5.3 (next page) shows the

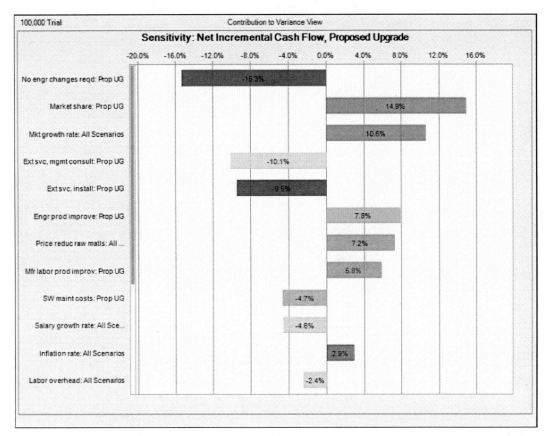

Exhibit 5.3 Sensitivity analysis for one financial metric, net incremental cash flow, from an incremental cash flow statement in the Aerofirma example. Figures in the cash flow statement actually derive from hundreds of assumptions, but sensitivity analysis showed the twelve listed here as the most important. These twelve will be discussed in the Recommendations and Conclusions Section of the report. All other assumptions will be noted simply in a report appendix.

Monte Carlo sensitivity analysis for one of the Aerofirma examples, the incremental cash flow statement for the Proposed Upgrade scenario. Here, the output value of interest is "net incremental cash flow," a financial metric derived from hundreds of assumptions. However, sensitivity analysis showed that only the twelve assumptions seen here have a significant influence on the output value. (The full financial model behind the cash flow statements, with its many assumptions is not shown here). These findings, too, will contribute to practical suggestions for management in the **Conclusions and Recommendations Section**.

Risk Analysis

The figures in the cash flow statements are the author's "most likely" or expected values. Everyone knows, however, that in reality these figures will almost certainly differ from the predicted values—either by a little or by a lot. It is important to ask: How likely is "most likely?" And how likely are other financial results? Could anything happen that would cause very different results? **Risk analysis** addresses such questions.

One simple, commonly used approach to risk analysis is to ask the business case author (perhaps in consultation with subject matter experts) to identify risk factors that might threaten expected results. Each risk is then rated subjectively on two components:

- Probability of occurring (high, medium or low).
- Impact importance (high, medium, or low).

A proposed action that comes with high probability, high impact risk factors might be viewed as a poor choice for implementation, while an action with only low probability, low impact risk factors might look like a better choice. This approach is better than no risk analysis at all if the author can (1) explain credibly why the risk probability is rated high, medium or low, and (2) explain what "Impact importance" means in tangible terms.

A more powerful and less subjective approach to risk analysis is available, however, if the author has already set up a sensitivity analysis for Monte Carlo simulation, as illustrated above. The examples above show how the simulation works with a spreadsheet model—where outputs are derived from input assumptions—to show sensitivity information (Exhibits 5.2 and 5.3). While the simulation program measures each assumption's contribution to the output, however, it also measures the probabilities of different outputs. To show what this information looks like, and what it can mean to decision makers and planners, it will be helpful first to show how probabilities enter the simulation.

Probabilities for Assumptions

The Monte Carlo simulation takes a set of input assumptions (such as the "Expected Values in rows 1-6 of Exhibit 5.1) and replaces all of them with new values, then checks to see what happened to the output value. That process is repeated over and over. The sensitivity information essentially represents the statistical correlation between each assumption and the output, measured over thousands of trials (as seen in Exhibits 5.2 and 5.3).

When the simulation program selects new assumption values, the selection follows certain rules. First, each new value must be within the range specified by "Min" and "Max" values for the assumption. Secondly, the selection of new values is *random*, a term that means "according to probability rules" (random does not mean "haphazard" or "unpredictable" as some people think).

The ranges, expected values, and probability rules for each assumption are specified by the author before running the simulation. That is done by describing the basic characteristics of a

Exhibit 5.4 Probability distributions chosen by the Aerofirma author for three of the six assumptions in the model for estimating initial training costs (Exhibit 5.1). See text for explanation.

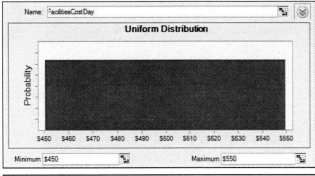

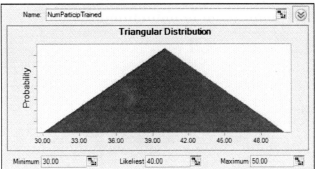

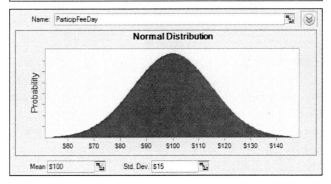

probability distribution for each assumption. Exhibit 5.4 (above) shows how the author set up 3 of the 6 assumptions for the initial training costs simulation. Note that the complete set of assumptions in the entire 3-scenario business case included several hundred assumptions (Exhibit 5.3 listed only the 12 assumptions scoring highest in the sensitivity analysis).

- For the assumption "facilities cost per day" (upper panel), the author was confident that a minimum of $450 and maximum of $550 covered all possibilities. The judgement may reflect experience with previous training events, or perhaps quoted rates from likely facilities providers. The rectangular probability distribution over this range means that, at this time, the author had no reason to expect any price in the range to be more likely than any other. The $500 figure was used for the cash flow statement training cost, simply because it is the mid point of this range.

- For the assumption "number of participants trained," (middle panel) the author was confident that a minimum of 30 and a maximum of 50 covered all possibilities. Discussions with the training manager and engineering manager, however, suggested that the extreme values of this range were unlikely, and that the actual number would be close to the "likeliest" value of 40. In such cases, the triangular distribution is appropriate.

- For the assumption "participant training fee per day" (lower panel) the author had enough information about likely values to specify that a normal distribution (Gaussian bell-shaped curve) appropriately described the likelihood of cost values. Here the curve is specified by a mean and standard deviation rather than a range. However, a normal distribution with a mean of $100 and a standard deviation of $15 puts 99.9% of the curve over the given range $50 - $150.

When the simulation program runs, all assumptions contribute some of their own uncertainty (variability) to overall uncertainty in the output results [2]. When each input uncertainty is defined with a range and a probability distribution, as shown, the input uncertainties are measurable. This means that the output uncertainty, which is the sum of the uncertainties contributed by input assumptions, can be measured as well.

Risk Analysis With Monte Carlo Simulation

The probability curves in Exhibit 5.4 describe uncertainty for individual input assumptions. Two panels in Exhibit 5.5 (next page) shows the resulting uncertainty in overall output results for the training cost example.

Remember that the predicted initial training cost figure was $108,000. In the upper panel, however, you can see that some simulation trials produced estimates well under $60,000, and on a few other trials, the cost estimate was well over $180,000. The dark shaded area, however, stands over the central 80% of the distribution. Now, the author can predict with 80% confidence that the actual initial training cost will be between $83,498 and $150,000. That kind of information is much more useful to management than a single point estimate that says the most likely figure is $108,000.

At Aerofirma, management had already set a budget limit of $120,000 for the initial training. With this in mind, the estimated figure of $108,000 sounded acceptable. But the very wide 80% confidence interval made them think again (the difference between upper and lower limits of the interval is $66,562). The lower panel shows the same probabilities plotted as a reverse

---

2. In statistical terms, the probability distributions in Exhibit 5.4 are *probability density functions* and the assumption values are *random variables*. When an interval, or segment of the horizontal axis is specified, the probability that an assumption falls inside the interval equals the proportion of the total area under the curve that stands over the interval. Documentation for Crystal Ball and other popular simulation programs provides guidance in selecting the appropriate distributions for assumptions, even for people with little or no background in statistics. If the author has no ability to suggest any particular distribution as appropriate for an assumption, the rectangular distribution may be used for all assumptions. The rectangular distribution adds more uncertainty (variability) to overall results than other distributions, but in the absence of more knowledge about the assumption, that is appropriate.

Exhibit 5.5. The probabilities of different initial training costs for the Aerofirma Example. The spreadsheet model in Exhibit 5.1 produced an estimated cost figure of $108,000 but Monte Carlo simulation with the same model shows that a wide range of other results are possible.

The upper panel shows the 80% confidence interval for the cost figure, $83,498-$150,000.

The lower figure shows that the probability of exceeding the training budget ($120,000) is 44.6%.

The single point estimate $108,000 may at first sound acceptable, but the very large uncertainty shown here, and the relatively high risk of exceeding budget, may make management less ready to approve the proposal as planned.

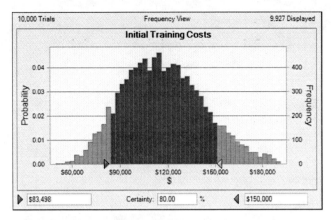

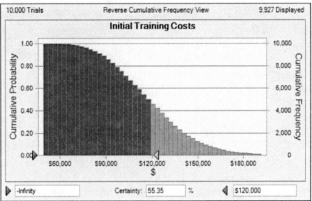

cumulative curve, which shows the probability of reaching or exceeding any cash flow result on the horizontal axis. Here, the probability of exceeding $120,000 is 44.6%. After reviewing these results, the author decided to take proactive steps to reduce the training cost estimate and its uncertainty (see "Maximizing Results and Minimizing Uncertainty, below). The author also provide some very practical guidance to management on these issues in the **Conclusions and Recommendations Section.**

Analysis of Full Value vs. Incremental Cash Flow Results

When management addresses planning questions, the risk and sensitivity analysis will focus on inputs and outputs for the full value cash flow statements. Questions about predicted sales revenues and funding requirements, for instance, are planning questions that look to the full value statements. The training cost example above, is concerned with a funding question. Management needs to know how much the company will actually spend—the full value.

Decision support questions, however, may focus more on the inputs and outputs to the incremental cash flow statements. Here, the purpose may be to recommend one scenario over

Exhibit 5.6. Monte Carol risk analysis for two scenarios in the Aerofirma example case. The upper panel shows probabilities for different values of incremental cash flow from the Proposed Upgrade scenario, while the bottom panel shows the same for the Combination Proposal scenario.

Both scenarios show similar expected net cash flow, similar NPV, and similar ROI metrics.

Expected results in the Combination Proposal scenario, however, come with much more uncertainty, meaning that scenario is much "riskier." The 90% confidence interval for the Proposed Upgrade Scenario covers a range of $18,269,000, while the 90% interval for the Combination Proposal covers a range of $28,033,000 in incremental cash flow.

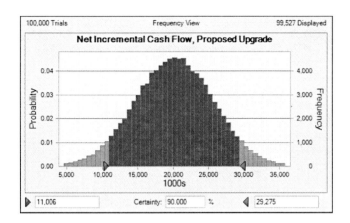

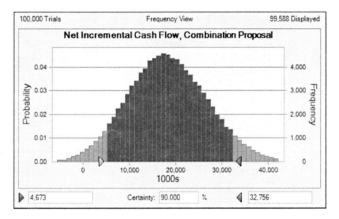

others for implementation. Important management questions ask how each proposal scenario compares to business as usual results. Results or objectives described as cost saving or avoided costs, for instance appear *only* on the incremental cash flow statement. The same is true for objectives described in relative terms, such "increase," "decrease" or "improvement."

In comparing the Aerofirma Proposed Upgrade Scenario with the Combination Proposal, for example, the full value cash flow statements show much higher 3-year projected benefits for the Combination over the Upgrade scenario: about $165 million vs. $146 million. However, the Combination scenario also comes with higher total 3-year costs, about $70 million vs. $49 million. In terms of projected cash flow, which scenario promises the better result? Does one scenario comes with higher risks than the other?

The most direct approach to such questions comes through analyzing the incremental cash flow statements. Exhibit 5.6 (above) shows the risk analysis for two scenarios in the Aerofirma example case. The upper panel shows incremental cash flow probabilities for the Proposed Upgrade scenario, while the bottom panel shows the same for the Combination Proposal scenario. Both proposal scenarios show similar net incremental cash flow, similar NPV, and similar ROI metrics. However, the Combination scenario appears much riskier. The 90% confidence interval for the Proposed Upgrade covers a range of $18,269,000, while the same interval for the

Combination Proposal covers a range of $28,033 in incremental cash flow. The riskiness of the Combination scenario outcomes will weigh against it in the author's **Conclusions and Recommendations Section.**

Maximizing Results and Minimizing Uncertainty

The business case analysis should be managed as a living document: updates and improvements should continue before and after the formal report is submitted for review and judgement.

In the Aerofirma example case, for instance, the author's first analysis of initial training costs produced a high expected value ($108,000) and a high level of uncertainty (an 80% confidence interval width of $66,562, and a 44.6% probability of exceeding the $120,000 training budget).

Sensitivity analysis shows how those involved with the case can improve this picture. The previous analysis found that the three most important input assumptions are also the three input values that management can control: Number of participants trained, class duration, and maximum class size (Exhibit 5.2). The author, therefore, undertook more research and discussion with the training manager, the training vendor, and the engineering manager, in an attempt to improve the expected cost value and the uncertainty that comes with it.

Exhibit 5.7 (below) summarizes the changes the author felt justified in making after these discussions:

- **Number of participants trained**. Based on a new review of skills in the Engineering department and a careful analysis of likely turnover in the next three years, the author, engineering manager, and training manager, agreed to adjust the expected number of participants trained from 40 down to 35. They agreed, moreover, to change the new "maximum trained" estimate from 50 to 40.

Assumptions (Uncertainties)	Assumption Names	Min	Expected Value	Max	
1 Number of partcipants trained	NumParticipTrained	30	40	50	Input assumptions, as entered for first analysis.
3 Class duration (Days)	ClassDuration	6	10	14	
4 Maximum class size	MaxClassSize	7	10	14	
1 Number of partcipants trained	NumParticipTrained	30	35	40	Input assumptions, as modified for second analysis.
3 Class duration (Days)	ClassDuration	7	8	9	
4 Maximum class size	MaxClassSize	7	12	12	
2 Instructor salary per day ($)	InstSalaryDay	$1,000	$1,200	$1,500	Input assumptions, unchanged from first analysis.
5 Participant training fee per day ($)	ParticipFeeDay	$60	$100	$150	
6 Facilites cost per pay ($)	FacilitiesCostDay	$450	$500	$600	
7 Instructor cost per class ($)	InstCostClass		$9,600		= InstSalaryDay * ClassDuration
8 Cost per participant ($)	ParticipCost		$800		= ClassDuration * ParticipFeeDay
9 Number of classes	NumClasses		3		= ROUNDUP (NumParticipTrained/MaxClassSize, 0)
10 Training facilities cost per class ($)	FacilCostClass		$4,000		= ClassDuration * FacilitiesCostDay
Total participant costs ($)	TotalParticipCosts		$28,000		= ParticipCost * NumParticipTrained
Total instructor costs $)	TotalInstCost		$28,800		= InstCostClass * NumClasses
Total Training Facility Costs ($)	TotalTrainFacilCosts		$12,000		= FacilCostClass * NumClasses
Initial Training Costs			$68,800		= TotalParticipCosts +TotalInstCost+TotalTrainFacilCosts

Exhibit 5.7 Modeling initial training costs from assumptions. This extract from a spreadsheet model is similar to Exhibits 4.6 and 5.1. In this instance, three of the assumptions have been modified in an attempt to lower the overall cost estimate and reduce uncertainty in predicted results.

Exhibit 5.8. Risk analysis for the initial training cost item after changing assumptions, as shown in Exhibit 5.7.

Compared to similar results in Exhibit 5.5, the expected cost has now dropped from $108,000 to $68,800, and the 80% confidence interval has narrowed by 36% over the earlier version (upper panel).

The lower panel shows that the probability of exceeding the $120,000 budget figure has dropped to virtually 0.

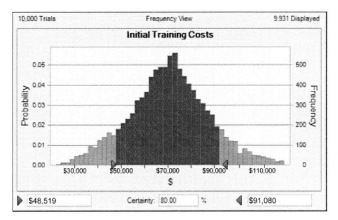

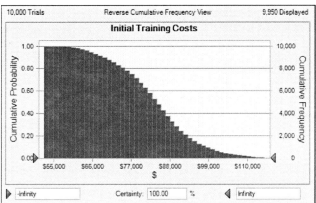

- **Class duration**. The author, training manager, and vendor also made a second review of training requirements, focusing more carefully on the actual number of training days that would be required. When they were confident that training could be completed in 8 classroom days, they adjusted the expected value for that assumption to 8. With a better understanding of training time requirements, they also changed the minimum estimated training time to 7 days and the maximum to 9.
- **Maximum class size.** The author and training manager also agreed that it was possible to find a training facility that accommodates more than 10 participants per class. They adjusted the expected maximum class size to 12, and set the range of possible class size maximum values to 7 - 12 (the range had been 7 - 14).

It is very important to remember that no one should make such changes simply in order to improve analysis results, unless the changes are fully justified by new research, new information, or changing conditions. These changes—if justified—make a dramatic improvement in the outlook for the training cost item. The estimated most likely value is now reduced 36% below its original value, from $108,000 to $68,800 (Exhibit 5.7, previous page). The 80% confidence interval for this value has now dropped to 64% of its former width, and the probability of exceeding the training budget ceiling of $120,000 is virtually zero (Exhibit 5.8, previous page).

Sensitivity and Risk Analysis for Non Financial Benefits and Costs

In many cases, non financial benefits and costs are as important or more important than the financial results in the eyes of those responsible for using the case. Expected non financial results, however, also predict the future, and that means they, too come with uncertainty. When the **Business Results Section** has presented important non financial results, these too should be subject to risk and sensitivity analysis. Those who use the business case need to know how likely these results are, how likely are other results, and which assumptions are most important in controlling these outcomes.

By this point in the business case report, the author should have established the legitimacy of any non financial benefits or costs that may be important, shown how they are measured, and connected them to business objectives. This would have been done in the **Methods** and **Business Results Sections**. Exhibit 5.9 (next page) illustrates some kinds of non financial outcomes that may be important to the case, and if so, need treatment here in the **Sensitivity and Risk Analysis Section**.

In dealing with non financial benefits and costs, remember that the benefit and the business objective that gives it value may in fact be two different outcomes, as suggested by the examples in Exhibit 5.9. Predicting the benefit's contribution to the objective depends on assumptions, but the assumptions and outcomes are not so easily handled with quantitative analysis like Monte Carlo simulation. Nevertheless, for non financial benefits and costs, the basic risk and sensitivity questions can still be asked and answered.

The risk and sensitivity discussion for non financial benefits and costs will build on the business results presented for these outcomes. Exhibit 4.9 (p. 69), for instance, showed how one author made the connection between shorter customer wait time on a call center phone line (the benefit), and improved customer satisfaction (the business objective). When addressing risk and sensitivity questions, the author should at a minimum explain:

- Which assumptions are most important in connecting the benefit or cost outcome with the business objective?
- Which of these assumptions are uncertain, or unproven? Which are relatively certain?
- What are the risk factors that could reduce the benefit or cost contribution? How likely are they?
- What is the maximum likely contribution to the objective? What is the minimum likely contribution?

	Organization	Business Benefit /Cost from Proposed Initiative	Business Objective Targeted
Non Financial Benefits	Manufacturing company, private industry	Shorter customer wait time on call center phone	Improved customer satisfaction
	Government Human Services Department	More case worker hours per client made available	Improved quality of social services delivered
	Defense Department	Lower maintenance requirements and higher reliability for weapons system	Improved readiness of military unit
	Secondary education system	Improved instruction in mathematics	Improved placement rate for graduates in high quality universities
	Government Transportation Department	Improved signals and lighting at dangerous intersections	Lower rates of highway fatalities and injuries
	Fashion designer, private industry	Celebrity endorsements	Improved brand image
Non Financial Costs	Financial services company, private industry	Lower employee pay raises resulting in lower employee morale	Lower operating expenses, reduced pressure on cash flow
	IT vendor, private industry	Lower customer satisfaction after call center service outsourced to lower quality provider	Lower costs of warranty service delivery

Exhibit 5.9. Example non financial benefits and costs and the business objectives they impact. Non financial outcomes cannot always be approached Monte Carlo simulation, like financial benefits and costs, but they are still subject to the same risk and sensitivity questions, and deserve the same kinds of answers.

Chapter 5 Summary

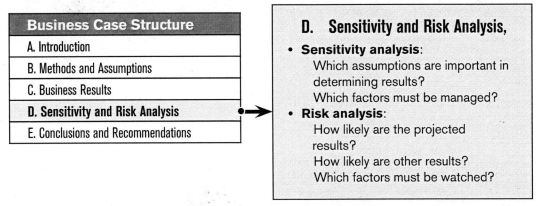

Business Case Structure
A. Introduction
B. Methods and Assumptions
C. Business Results
D. Sensitivity and Risk Analysis
E. Conclusions and Recommendations

D. Sensitivity and Risk Analysis,
- **Sensitivity analysis**:
  Which assumptions are important in determining results?
  Which factors must be managed?
- **Risk analysis**:
  How likely are the projected results?
  How likely are other results?
  Which factors must be watched?

- The Business Results section presents the author's estimated most likely outcomes. In reality, however, an infinite number of other outcomes are also possible. Those responsible for using the case need to know which assumptions are most important in determining results and the likelihood of different results appearing.

- Sensitivity analysis shows which assumptions are most important in controlling business case results, and how much those results change when the assumptions change.

- Sensitivity analysis requires the author to specify a range of possible values for each assumption rather than a single point estimate. Sensitivity analysis also requires a dynamic financial model, in which input assumptions work together to produce output values.

- In simple sensitivity analysis, assumptions which cause the larger changes in output are identified as more powerful than those that cause smaller changes.

- Sensitivity analysis with Monte Carlo simulation measures statistical relationships between assumptions and outputs. The most important assumptions are identified by their high correlation with changes in output results.

- Monte Carlo simulation also provides risk analysis, that is, a measure of the probabilities associated with different outcomes. With risk analysis, the author may be able to make statements like this: "The 90% confidence interval for net cash flow is $10 million - $14 million."

- Budgeting and planning questions are usually addressed by analyzing the full value cash flow statements. Scenario comparisons, for the purpose of choosing one scenario to recommend over others, are usually addressed through analysis of incremental cash flow statements.

- Sensitivity and risk analysis can also provide the information necessary for management to maximize returns, reduce costs, and minimize uncertainty in projected business outcomes.

- Insofar as possible, the author should also address the basic risk and sensitivity questions for important non financial costs and benefits.

Chapter 6
Conclusions and Recommendations

Building blocks in this section address issues that were raised initially in the introductory sections of the business case report. Much of the preceding material intends to "let the numbers speak for themselves," but the final sections of the report interpret the numbers and connect them to objectives, decisions, and actions.

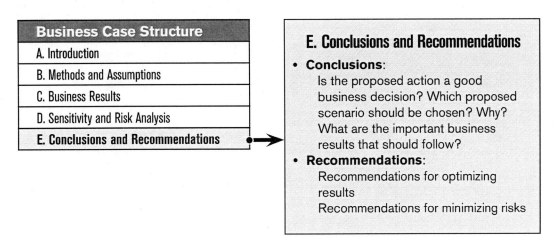

It is rarely safe to assume that readers will read the business results and analyses and automatically draw the same conclusions as the author. Nor can the author assume they will immediately grasp what needs to be done in order to ensure that predicted results arrive. The **Conclusions and Recommendations Section** completes the case, by stating the author's conclusions, supporting them with evidence from the preceding sections, and recommending in practical terms what must be done in order to maximize results and minimize risks. This section will be very weak if it is nothing more than a simple list of major financial projections.

Conclusions

Business case conclusions are written with the case purpose and subject in mind. The **Purpose Statement** in the **Introduction Section** (pp. 17-19) outlines clearly who is going to use the case, for what purpose, and what information they need in order to meet that purpose. The **Subject Statement** (pp. 13-17) describes what is proposed and the business objectives addressed by the proposal. The **Situation** block (pp. 19-20) explains why the objectives addressed are important. Here, the **Conclusions** block "makes the case" by pointing directly back to these earlier blocks.

The purpose statement of the Aerofirma example case, for instance, begins by identifying who is going to use the case and for what purpose:

This analysis and report are prepared for the members of Aerofirma Executive Management Committee, who will meet in December 2009 to decide whether or not to implement upgrades to Aerofirma's primary engineering software system and other proposed changes in Engineering and Manufacturing. Options for action include the three scenarios evaluated in this case:

1. Proposed Upgrade Scenario: Upgrade engineering design software system.
2. Combination Proposal: Upgrade design software, reorganize engineering workgroups improve manufacturing set up process.
3. Business as usual (implement none of the proposed actions).

The purpose statement goes on to identify specific criteria the committee will look to, when deciding which scenario to implement. These criteria include specific financial metrics, as well as marketing, sales, operational, and performance metrics, and risks. The conclusion section presents the author's conclusions about this decision, based on these criteria. This is meant to be the essence of what decision makers need to know to choose one scenario over another.

Conclusions

Based on a comparison of expected business results under all three scenarios considered, the Proposed Upgrade Scenario represents the best business decision for Aerofirma.

1. Predicted 3-year net incremental cash flow is greatest under the Proposed Upgrade Scenario: Net cash flow is
   – $20,558 greater than Business as Usual under the Proposed Upgrade Scenario.
   – $19,186 greater than Business as Usual under the Combination Proposal Scenario.

2. Uncertainty in predicted net cash flow is much less under Proposed Upgrade compared to the Combination Proposal. Simulation analysis shows a 90% confidence interval width of
   –$18,269 million for the Proposed Upgrade Scenario.
   –$28,033 for the Combination Proposal.

3. Both proposal scenarios predict increases in Aerofirma gross profits, by reaching our targets for increased Market Share, margins, and number of new products developed. The Proposed Upgrade Scenario predicts 3-year gross profits of $145.8 million, while the Combination Proposal predicts gross profits of $164.5 million. However the greater gross profits under the Combination Proposal also come with greater expected costs—the reason that incremental cash flow is higher under the Proposed Upgrade Scenario (No. 1 above).

4. Both proposal scenarios show attractively high anticipated 3-year Return on Investment (ROI): 432% ROI for the Proposed Upgrade Scenario vs. 378% ROI for the Combination Proposal. The Combination Proposal ROI, however, comes with slightly more uncertainty than the estimated Proposal Scenario ROI.

5. Both proposal scenarios anticipate reducing design change costs, as targeted. Compared to Business as Usual, Estimated 3-year change cost reductions are:
   –$12.7 million reduction under the Proposed Upgrade Scenario
   –$12.8 million reduction the Combination Proposal Scenario
   Again, however, the estimated Combination Proposal figures comes with the same disadvantage in greater uncertainty and higher overall costs compared to the Proposal Scenario.

6. Anticipated avoided costs for Engineering labor are essentially the same under both proposal scenarios, about $7.7 million over three years, compared to Business as Usual.

7. Both proposal scenarios anticipate achieving targeted reductions in average design time for products and manufacturing set up time.

The **Conclusions** block is also the place to point out any surprising or unexpected results of the analysis and to discuss any findings that could be misinterpreted.

Recommendations

The author's conclusions are more compelling if they are accompanied by a **Recommendations** block that provides concrete, practical guidance on how to maximize results and minimize uncertainty for the recommend action.

The author's recommendations will depend heavily on the results of risk and sensitivity analysis. The Sensitivity analysis, for instance shows which assumptions are most important in determining predicted results. You may recall the Aerofirma example, where overall cash flow results were the product of hundreds of assumptions, but sensitivity analysis showed that just six of them, together accounted for most of the results variability (Exhibit 5.3, p. 73).

1. Assumed reduction in engineering change orders per year under the proposal scenario.
2. Assumed growth in Aerofirma market share.
3. Assumed growth in Aerofirma market size.
4. Assumed cost of migration and systems integration services.
5. Assumed cost of management consulting services.
6. Assumed productivity increase of design engineers with the upgraded design system.

You may also recall, that when these six assumptions emerged from the sensitivity analysis as the most important, the Author returned to the **Methods and Assumptions Section** of the report and inserted them under the heading "Major Assumptions." This alerts readers to the important role these assumptions play in explaining results and in managing the action once implementation begins. As suggested in Exhibit 6.1 (next page), the **Recommendations** block should recognize that important assumptions fall into two categories:

1. Assumptions about factors that are completely outside management control. These might include assumptions about such things as: the rate of inflation, competitor's actions, foreign currency exchange rates, prices of raw materials, the impact of weather, natural disasters, acts of war, or government regulation.

   These assumptions are designated as *risks*. The author will advise management to watch these factors carefully, and to expect different business results if they change.

2. Assumptions about factors that can be influenced or controlled to some degree. These might include such things as: skill levels of the professional staff, timely completion of related projects, achieving cost control goals, recruitment and hiring of key individuals, and many others.

   These assumptions are designated as *critical success factors* (CSFs), or *contingencies*, that must be managed to target levels in order to achieve predicted business results.

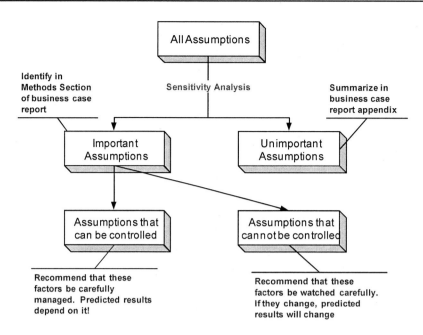

Exhibit 6.1. Risk and sensitivity analysis provide the basis for developing useful, practical recommendations for management. Analysis first shows which assumptions are important in determining business results and which are not. The important assumptions are further divided into two groups: Those that can be controlled to some extent by, and those that cannot. Those that can be controlled, and managed to target levels, are highlighted as critical success factors, or contingencies. Important assumptions that cannot be controlled are risk factors that must be watched carefully during implementation.

When the author recommends to management that an assumption has to be managed to target level, or that a risk should be watched carefully, it is helpful to display additional output from the simulation-based risk and sensitivity analysis, such as the tornado chart and spider charts in Exhibit 6.2 (next page). These examples also came from the simulation with the Proposed Upgrade Scenario incremental cash flow model, and they carry essentially the same message presented in the simple sensitivity analysis (Exhibit 5.2, p. 76): They show how much improvement or loss management can expect by changing each assumption through most of its possible range.[1]

1. The tornado chart and spider chart analyses look very similar to the results of simple sensitivity analysis (Exhibit 5.2, p. 76). Many people ask "What's the difference?" The answer is based in statistics: these analyses have more predictive validity than the simple sensitivity analysis. In the simple analysis, each assumption was tested at minimum, expected, and maximum values. Here, each assumption is tested over thousands of trials, and the predictive results are shown across a range of *percentile* values. The percentiles refer to percentile rank within each assumption's distribution of potential values—which takes into account the probability distribution and the range for the assumption. One result of this can be seen in the spider chart: the spider's "arms" are not straight lines, as in the simple sensitivity chart. In reality, of course, many people prefer to use the simple sensitivity analysis at this point because it is simpler, easier to apply, and easier to understand. But in cases where the author can apply Monte Carlo simulation, the approach shown here provides better predictions of each assumption's contribution to changing results.

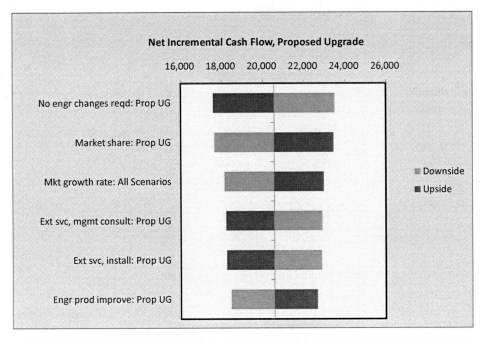

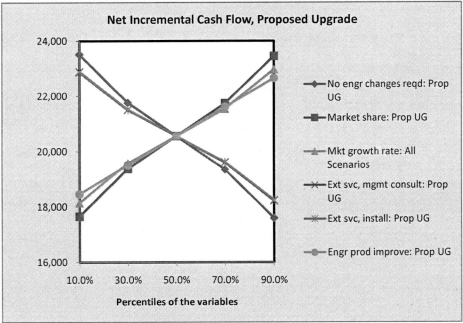

Exhibit 6.2. Tornado chart (top panel) and spider chart (lower panel) developed by Monte Carlo simulation during risk and sensitivity analysis. These results are for the Aerofirma Proposed Upgrade incremental cash flow model. The results here is look very similar to the simple sensitivity analysis presented in Exhibit 5.2. The charts show how much the incremental cash flow will increase or decrease as each of the important assumptions change.

With such information to draw from, the author's **Recommendations** block in the Aerofirma case will include SIX specific recommendations. One of these, the recommendation for change order reduction might look like this:

Change Order Reduction.

The potential for cost savings through lower change order costs is large, estimated at $12.7 million across 3 years when the recommended Proposed upgrade scenario is compared to Business as Usual. This figure assumes reductions in the annual number of change orders, and the movement of relatively more of the remaining changes into earlier design stages.

If anticipated change order improvements reach only 50% of the expected improvement level, the cost to Aerofirma (relative to projected results) would be a reduction in net incremental cash flow of about 6.0 million across 3 years. If, however, the reduction in change costs *exceeds* the expected level by 20%, the contribution to increased incremental cash flow would be about $1.0 million.

Reaching targeted levels of change order reduction will depend heavily on design engineer ability to exploit the analytic power of the upgraded design system, to reduce design errors such as clashes, and to anticipate change needs earlier in earlier design. Experience shows that these skills are best learned and improved under the guidance of a senior engineer with deep experience in change prevention and change management.

Accordingly, it is recommended that an Aerofirma Senior engineer with these qualifications be appointed "Change Improvement Manager," for the first year of implementation, with the primary responsibility of achieving the targeted improvements for the engineering organization by the end of the year.

Note that this recommendation (and the others not shown here) should be about meeting business objectives. The whole case, in fact, is about meeting business objectives and, as shown throughout this book, business objectives are the primary concern in each section and building block in the case.

Chapter 6 Summary

Business Case Structure
A. Introduction
B. Methods and Assumptions
C. Business Results
D. Sensitivity and Risk Analysis
E. Conclusions and Recommendations

E. Conclusions and Recommendations

- **Conclusions**:
  Is the proposed action a good business decision? Which proposed scenario should be chosen? Why? What are the important business results that should follow?
- **Recommendations**:
  Recommendations for optimizing results
  Recommendations for minimizing risks

- The Conclusions and Recommendations Section completes the case by stating the author's s conclusions, supporting them with evidence from the preceding sections, and recommending in practical terms what must be done in order to maximize results and minimize risks.

- The author's conclusions should be organized around the main points in the subject and the purpose statements from the Introduction Section. Conclusions should refer directly to the business objectives addressed by the actions (subject statement) and the decision criteria and other important information required by decision makers and planners (purpose statement).

- Sensitivity analysis provides a basis for making practical, useful recommendations. Sensitivity analysis first identifies the assumptions that are most important in determining business case results. These important assumptions fall into two categories:

  - Those assumptions about factors that are completely outside management control. These assumptions are designated as *risks*. The author will advise management to watch these factors carefully, and to expect different business results if they change.

  - Those assumptions which can be influenced or controlled to some degree.
    These assumptions are designated as *critical success factors* (CSFs), or *contingencies*, that must be managed to target levels in order to achieve predicted business results.

Index

Further Information

For More Information

The contents of this book are covered in more detail in the book *The Business Case Guide* (ISBN 978-1-929500-05-5). For more information on the *Guide* please visit www.solutionmatrix.com/guide

Copyright

About the Author

Marty J. Schmidt is founder and President of Solution Matrix Ltd. Dr. Schmidt has twenty years business experience, managing software development, international marketing and sales support, and management consulting on business planning. He is a recognized authority on the application of cost/benefit analysis and business case development.

Dr. Schmidt also taught graduate and undergraduate statistics at the University of New Hampshire. He is also the author of *The Business Case Guide, Understanding and Using Statistics* (a college textbook on applied statistics), and publishes often on professional management and business issues. He holds the Ph.D. degree from Purdue University and the M.B.A. from Babson College.

About Solution Matrix Limited

Solution Matrix Ltd. is a management consulting firm dedicated to helping executives, managers, consultants, and other professionals understand the impact of management actions on business performance. Solution Matrix clients include individuals and organizations on five continents, in business, government, education, the military, and non profit organizations. For more information on our products and services, visit www.solutionmatrix.com. For the latest schedule of "Building the Business Case" seminar offerings visit www.solutionmatrix.com/seminar.